THE
COWBOY HAT
BOOK

William Reynolds & Ritch Rand

Gibbs Smith, Publisher
Salt Lake City

Acknowledgments

Hats may have their own stories, but a book like this needs to evolve. Evolution takes time and effort, and both were expended by many who Ritch and I wish to thank.

Joanne Hale, James Nottage, and Susan DeLand of the Gene Autry Western Heritage Museum for their assistance and gracious western attitudes in providing us access to the fabulous hats from the museum's collection and for the use of Mr. Autry's hand-colored photo on the front cover of this book.

Coauthor Ritch Rand for the use and display of his collection of promotional western feature photographs.

Phil Spangenberger for the use of his extensive collection of historical western stills throughout the book.

Gregory Peterson and Studio 7 for their photographs and photographic skills in capturing the "essence of great head wear."

The many professional "hatters," manufacturers, and individuals who either contributed to the project or taught us by example: Peter H. Annunziata of *Hat Life*, Robert S. Stec, Doug Patton, Bob Posey, Gordon Moore, Chip Alexander, Bill Stein, Curt Glass, Heather Harding, Tom Hurt, Mike Malone, Ron Barrow, Letitia Glenn, Kevin O'Farrell, Buck Brannaman, Ian Tyson, William Matthews, Don Hedgpeth, Chas Weldon, Chuck Stormes, Joe Beeler, Bob Brand, David Roll, Russ Besold, Rod Patrick, Tab Sparks, Gary Epstein, Lindsey and Nancy Enderby of Horse Feather Store, Taos, New Mexico.

Our helpers who assisted in crafting the visual and verbal package: graphic designer Roger Mejia of Banning Co., Inc. in Los Angeles and copyeditor Tyler Baldwin for their tireless effort.

Finally, we wish to thank our editors, Dawn Valentine Hadlock and Madge Baird, for their patience and sensitive handling of us, and publisher, Gibbs Smith, who entertained the idea in the first place.

Revised edition 2003 11 10 09 08 8 7 6 5 4
Text © 1995, 2003 by William Reynolds and Ritch Rand
Unless otherwise credited, all photographs ©1995, 2003
by William Reynolds

Published by
Gibbs Smith
P.O. Box 667
Layton, Utah 84041
Orders: (1-800) 748-5439
www.gibbs-smith.com

Illustrations & Design by Roger Mejia of Banning Co., Inc.
Manufactured in Korea by Sung In Communications Co., Ltd.
Front and back cover photograph © 1995 by Gregory Peterson

Library of Congress Cataloging-in-Publication Data

Rand, Ritch, 1949-
    The cowboy hat book / written by Ritch Rand and William Reynolds.
        p.   cm.
    ISBN 10: 1-58685-258-2. – ISBN 13: 978-1-58685-258-0
    1. Cowboys--West (U.S.)– Costume. 2. Hats–West (U.S.)
I. Reynolds, Bill , 1950- . II. Title.   94-33734
F596. R36 1995   CIP
391'.43–dc20

The Cowboy Hat Book

Portrait of a Young Man,
Ben Johnson.
(Courtesy Ritch Rand.)

RIGHT: *Patriotic quill-and-beaded-band, laced-edge 5X from Jackson Hole Hats.*
(Courtesy of Studio Seven.)

Above: Hondo, the man.
(Courtesy of Ritch Rand.)

Hondo, the hat, a miniature salesman's sample
by Ritch Rand.
(Courtesy of Ritch Rand.)

Contents

Legendary photographer of Native Americans,
Edward S. Curtis dons a stylized hat which, as
his photography, was sophisticated and
individual for its era.
(Courtesy of Christopher Cardozo, Inc.)

Every hat holds a story,

and the experiences of the owner

show through with little explanation.

Al Seiber, U.S. Army
*Chief of Scouts during the last
Apache campaign (1885-86),
Seiber shows off his flat-
brimmed Stetson with a rather
rakish tassel. Al's wide-
brimmed felt hat is typical of
the neutral-colored type often
worn in the American
Southwest.*
(Courtesy of Phil Spangenberger Collection.)

My grandfather's Stetson rests on a shelf above me. R. C. Lawry wore his hat during the twenties and thirties, when he had the horse ranch outside of Tucson. That hat holds many of his great stories and memories—if it could only talk. There are no keys to unlock those tales, but the hat speaks of both good times and bad, in the sun and in the rain. The felt of the hat shows wear—wear from the passage of time, created and

sustained by remembered, treasured experiences outdoors and on horseback. All old cowboy hats speak of experience. Each tear, each crease says something about the owner–where he's been or what she's been through.

The older hats you'll see in this book reflect the experiences held within the well-worn and well-loved cowboy hat—experiences as wonderful as those kept within my grandfather's hat. Cowboy hats have been worn by kings and ranch hands, by celebrities, political figures, and businessmen alike. But one thing is certain—whoever you are, when that hat goes on your head, something unique happens. For a brief moment, you become a part of a grand adventure; you're transported into another time and space, when the West wasn't just a place, but an adventure, a state of mind.

The new hats shown within these pages show the hatters' art at its finest—an art and craft that has not changed over the last 100 years. It still takes over thirteen, highly-skilled artisans to make a cowboy hat—there are some things that are best not improved upon.

ABOVE: *R. C. and Betty Lawry**, lovers of the West and each other, The Flying V Ranch, Tuscon, Arizona, 1934.*
(Courtesy of Bill Reynolds.)

RIGHT: *Gen. George A. Custer* *is wearing a nonissue, privately purchased hat of the type favored by many cavalry officers during the Civil War.*
(Courtesy of Phil Spangenberger Collection.)

A LITTLE HISTORY

ABOVE: *Previously unpublished photo of Buffalo Bill and his Wild West Show in Scotland at the turn of the century. The photo shows the ladies were as "entered up" as men in their performing as well as their choice in "punchy" headwear.*
(Courtesy of Ritch Rand.)

There are few items in the history of American culture that carry the same iconic weight as the cowboy hat. It is the one item of apparel that can be worn in any corner of the world and receive immediate recognition. As the old cowboy saying goes, It's the last thing you take off and the first thing that is noticed.

The history of the cowboy hat is not that old. Before the invention of the cowboy hat (which means before John B. Stetson came along), the cowpunchers of the plains wore castoffs of previous lives and vocations. Everything, from formal top hats and derbies to leftover remnants of Civil War headgear to tams and sailor hats, was worn by men moving westward.

The cowboy hat is truly an example of form following function. Invented by John B. Stetson (the son of a Philadelphia hatmaker), today's cowboy hat has remained basically unchanged in construction and design since the first one was created in 1865. As the story goes, John B. Stetson and some companions went west to seek the benefits of a drier climate. During a hunting trip, Stetson amused his

friends by showing them how he could make cloth out of fur without weaving.

Stetson used the fur from hides collected on the hunting trip. Kneading the fur and working it with his hands, dipping it into boiling water, spreading it out, kneading it, and dipping it again, he created a soft, smooth piece of felt. Using a technique that has been known since the beginning of modern civilization, Stetson amazed his friends by using the only material he had at hand—fur.

Fur is essentially the hair of certain mammals and is

LEFT: *The notorious Belle Starr is seen here in her black velvet riding habit, a brace of Colt revolvers, and her wide-brimmed riding hat.*
(Courtesy of Ritch Rand.)

made of a series of little hooks and prongs. When stimulated by kneading and water, matting occurs, which causes the fur to hold on to itself. As the water dries up, the fur contracts and the little prongs and hooks draw closer and closer together as additional kneading is applied.

After creating his "fur blanket," Stetson fashioned an enormous hat with a huge brim as a joke, but the hat was noted to be big enough to protect a man from sun, rain, and all the rigors the outdoors could throw at him.

Stetson decided to wear the hat on his hunting trip, and it worked so well that he continued wearing it on his travels throughout the West. Later, he sold the hat to a rugged horseman who was fascinated by the unique headwear. Stetson received five dollars for his invention, and as he stood back and watched the horseman ride away with the hat perched on his head, a rather mythical sight struck him. The impressive image was not lost on Stetson, and when

he returned to Philadelphia, he pondered the potential of a piece of headwear that would protect its wearer from the elements.

In 1865, as the cattle business began to boom, Stetson became convinced that the cowmen of the West would see his new hat as a useful addition to their wardrobe. He began to produce the first incarnation of his "big hats" (originally called the Boss of the Plains) in number, and immediately dispatched samples to potential dealers throughout the West. As they say, "to make a long story short," Stetson was soon inundated with orders for the unique headgear. He even attracted the attention of the Texas Rangers, which quickly became the first law-enforcement group to use cowboy hats as part of its official uniform.

Before long, Stetson was considered the maker of this newfangled headwear, the cowboy hat. It had the unique capability, even in those early years, to identify its wearer as someone associated with the West, and that meant the cattle industry, whether he wore cowman's gear or not. Merely by placing his new cowboy hat on his head, he became part of a growing fraternity of cowmen who carried with them an image and aura intrinsically linked to the Wild West.

The cowboy hat rapidly became a regular and necessary part of the cowman's daily wear. The wide brim made quick work of fanning a fire. It could be used to whip a horse, wave to distant riders, and yes, even lend an air of grace and prestige to the man beneath its brim. And, of course, during inclement weather, the cowboy hat served as a very effective umbrella.

Beyond its utilitarian use around the ranch, the inclination to fill the crown made the hat a perfect hiding place, as well. It became the chosen spot for hiding money and important papers that would be unprotected elsewhere. As we all know, the first thing a cowboy puts on in the morning and the last thing he takes off at night is his hat; so, it was a natural place to keep his secrets and treasures, hence the phrase "keeping something under one's hat."

BELOW: *Buffalo Bill in a dapper moment. Bill Cody was a natty dresser and usually wore a broad-brimmed Stetson, both while performing and in his private life. Photo dates to around 1900.* (Courtesy of Ritch Rand.)

Left to the imagination, the cowboy hat became a valued addition to the wardrobe of any man of the West. Because of the tight weave of most Stetson hats, the concept of the "multigallon" hat came into play, as it was waterproof enough to be used as a bucket. Actually, the term ten-gallon did not originally refer to the holding capacity of the hat (the average hat held only a few quarts), but to the width of a Mexican sombrero hatband, and is more closely related to this unit of measurement by the Spanish than to the water-holding capacity of a Stetson.

Then, like today, a well-made cowboy hat was not inexpensive. In fact, the cowboy hat was considered to be a major investment. The original Stetson hat sold for five dollars. Today, hats of equal quality can sell for over one hundred dollars to upwards of one

ABOVE: These Oklahoma Territory lawmen sport a variety of hat styles of the 1890s era, from fairly narrow to broad-brimmed types. In typical Victorian fashion, they are all wearing ties. The Winchester lever rifles, shotgun, and Colt revolvers suggest they are out for business. (Courtesy of Herb Peck, Jr. Collection.)

ABOVE RIGHT: *This 1870s-era frontier scout, Hank Wormwood, wears a fringed buckskin shirt and pants, and carries an 1873 Winchester rifle and a Smith & Wesson .44 American revolver. His hat is a felt Mexican type with silken cords around the crown and probably silver bullion embroidery along the brim and crown.*
(Courtesy of Greg Silva Memorial Old West Archives Collection.)

LEFT: *This photograph, probably taken around 1860, shows a flamboyant frontiersman decked out in a brocaded vest, fringed linen hunting frock, muzzle-loading rifle, bowie knife, and an 1851 Navy Colt revolver. His hat is a common style of the period and was favored by those living in sunny climates, thus the wide brim—much like the plantation hats of the deep south.*
(Courtesy of Herb Peck, Jr. Collection.)

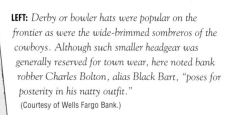

LEFT: *Derby or bowler hats were popular on the frontier as were the wide-brimmed sombreros of the cowboys. Although such smaller headgear was generally reserved for town wear, here noted bank robber Charles Bolton, alias Black Bart, "poses for posterity in his natty outfit."*
(Courtesy of Wells Fargo Bank.)

RIGHT: *This "posed" photo of gamblers on the frontier illustrates that even during the heat of the game, hats were not removed indoors. Note the wide grosgrain ribbon trim on the gamester at far right.*
(Courtesy of Phil Spangenberger Collection.)

THIS PAGE: *This pre-1889 classic photo illustrates a typical cowboy from the Montana Territories. He is wearing the favorite hat of the era–a J. B. Stetson "Boss of the Plains" with a "personalized" Montana pinch-front crease. This image has been the basis for many cowboy stereotype perceptions around the world.*
(Courtesy of Phil Spangenberger Collection.)

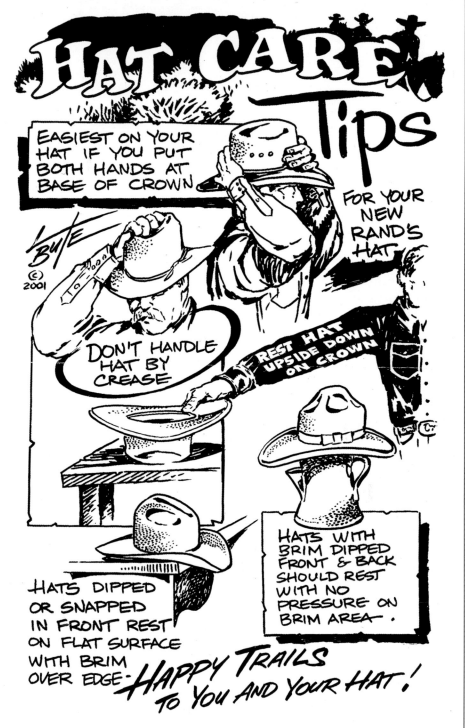

thousand dollars. Before the heyday of the cowboy (between 1860 and the end of the 1880s), Stetson hats made of fine beaver sold for anywhere from ten to thirty dollars. The irony is that the hat often cost more than an entire suit of clothing, and it wasn't unheard of for a man to spend a month's wages on a hat.

Shortly after the turn of the century, the cowboy hat, although still in its infancy, nevertheless infused its wearer with a singular link to the history of the wild and woolly West. Even after the "wild" aspect of the West was somewhat tamed, the cowboy hat never really lost its ability to lend that reckless and rugged aura to its wearer.

With the advent of the motion picture (and shortly thereafter, the silver-screen cowboy), the cowboy hat experienced a resurgence of popularity. Eager and impressionable audiences saw cowboy hats on the likes of Tom Mix, Bill Hart, and Ken Maynard. The romantic and rugged characters these actors

RIGHT: *This 1880s U.S. artilleryman is wearing the standard issue, tan felt campaign hat as issued from the early 1880s through the turn of the century. Unlike the movie military, the U.S. Army's official issue hats were generally of this type—not the broad-brimmed white hats so often seen on the silver screen.*
(Courtesy of Phil Spangenberger Collection.)

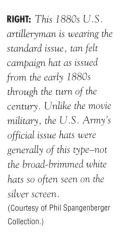

LEFT: *Typical headgear of the Old West sported wide, flat brims and large crowns that could be shaped by the wearer—often by a simple punch or dimple as seen here on this buckskinned frontiersman. He's also wearing the classic square-toed boots of the nineteenth century, and is brandishing his 1875 Remington six-shooter for the eastern folks to ogle.*
(Courtesy of Phil Spangenberger Collection.)

RIGHT: *Living legend, test pilot Chuck Yeager wearing his cowboy crown.*
(Courtesy of Ritch Rand.)

In many cases, attempts were made by ranch crews to recreate a "family crease," generally devised from the classic "cattleman three-crease" (two side creases and one top crease) with a longhorn brim, which were often found around the stockyards of Texas. It is the nature of the crease in the crown and the shape of the brim that creates a unique accent for the person wearing a particular hat. While styles come and go, crown heights and brim widths seem to vary only marginally with the passing of time.

Today, while there are many manufacturers involved in making both inexpensive wool and felt machine-blocked hats, as well as custom manufacturers making hand-creased magic, the basic hat remains the same. Its function continues—to protect its wearer from the blistering effects of the sun and the tortures of wind and rain. While some of today's hats remain true to their turn-of-the-century beginnings and others follow their own design features, today's cowboy hat continues to be seen as the last vestige of apparel of a young and untamed nation. It makes a statement about the tough individuality at the center of every pioneer that carved a life from the new frontier.

portrayed helped the cowboy hat and its wearer maintain a "wild and woolly" image.

In addition, there came to be a kind of code to the particular style, shape, and size of the cowboy hat. While it remained a universal image of the American West, certain nuances in shape, size, and style provided specific information to the wearer's background and geographic base. With a subtle adjustment to the brim and a couple of extra dents in the crown, a man could indicate that he was from the northern regions of Nevada or the rough plains of Texas, the wind-whipped ranges of the Rockies or the low deserts of New Mexico.

For example, in the high-desert reaches of northern Nevada, cowboy hats take on a rugged, historic look that seems to be a merging of the vaquero of California and the cowman of Texas. The hats worn by these riders of the scrub sage tend to carry a more surreal yet conservative look; crowns tend to be more open or simply dented in on the side; brims tend to be flat.

While John Stetson was able to create a cowboy hat using the most rudimentary tools and techniques, the hatter's art has been refined significantly through the years.

Fur

We begin with the specific material desired to create the hat—in nearly every case, fur felt. Felt differs from every other fabric in that it is made of thousands of short, single, animal-fur fibers, which tend to twist together when kneaded and manipulated in hot water and steam. Felt can be made into the smoothest fabric known (due to the interlocking action of the fibers) and the lightest fabric known (in relation to its tensile strength), because a minimum of fibers are required to create the necessary toughness. These factors also make felt one of the most resilient of fabrics and one of the fabrics most impervious to water, due to the close, interlocking fibers and the fact that animal fibers themselves do not soak up moisture.

Felt hats can be made of either fur felt (mid to high price range) or wool felt (low price range). The best and most durable hats are made with fur felt, which is composed primarily of rabbit fur or beaver fur. Some hare fur is used to make better hats, but beaver and nutria are usually used in the best hats. (Nutria is a South American animal similar to a large vole or small beaver.)

Beaver fur is still the most popular fur for felt hats. Pure, undyed beaver fur, known as "clear hair," is some of the better fur on the market. Beaver fur is very dense, holds its shape, has more oil, felts together tighter, and repels water better than blends or rabbit fur felt.

By "fur" we refer to the downy under-fur of these animals, not the long, coarse hair commonly known as "fur." Only this under-fur has barb-like projections on the surface of each fiber that will lock the fibers together to make a strong felt.

The long hairs are pulled out or sheared off, and the remaining under-fur is chemically treated to raise up the microscopic barbs for better felting. The under-fur is then cut from the skin and separated into grades of felt to be used for different qualities of hats.

Fur felt hats are superior in their lightness of weight and in their ability to keep their shape and withstand weather and renovating. A good fur blend encompasses large and small fibers, imparting smoothness and compactness. As many as eight different types or grades of fur may be used to create a single fur mixture.

The X-Factor

In the hatmaking field, felt has traditionally been graded according to its X-factor. The X-factor was originally determined by the density and shape of the material, and ranged in grade from a low of 1X to a high of 10X. Hats made of material rated below 5X generally contained a poorer grade of fur and little or no beaver fur. A 10X hat was made of 100% beaver fur. The X-factor was also a fairly reliable price guide, with a 3X hat costing $30, a 4X hat costing $40, a 5X hat costing $50, and so on. Fifty years ago, a 10X Stetson cost $100, was made of 100% pure beaver fur, and was the finest hat available.

Today, however, the X-factor rating system is rather subjective. Manufacturers and dealers are not only

rating hats differently, each according to its own criteria, but they are also using the X as a price plateau rather than an actual quality rating system. In general, today's X-factor works out like this: a 2X beaver will cost under $100; a 10X beaver about $250; a 30X, $450; and 100X beaver hats generally cost upwards of $1,000. One company's 5X beaver might actually be better than another's 10X—it's a

ABOVE: *Hatter forming hat shells.*
(Courtesy of Ritch Rand.)

LEFT: *Hatter is shown manually flattening brim for trimming. Photo circa 1930s. Note the hatter's headwear.*
(Courtesy of Bailey Hats.)

tricky system. Prospective hat buyers are advised to discuss the material's X-factor with the hatmaker or dealer in detail to ascertain the true X-rating. The real test, ultimately, is the look and feel: a good hat is soft and silky.

Shaping, Measuring, and Fitting

Once the felt has been manufactured, there are two main steps in making it into a hat. First, the material is shaped into a large, loose cone, or hood, by repeated stretching and moistening. The hood is then shrunk and shaped into the shell, which is then turned into the finished hat some thirteen steps later.

In making a custom hat, it is imperative to properly measure the customer's head and to discuss in detail the type of crease, taper, brim, crown height, etc., the customer wants. Once these variables have been decided upon, the hood can be formed with enough leeway to provide for the particular style and size requirements issued by the individual.

Creating the hood is one of the keys to felt hatmaking. It is done in a forming machine, which creates a fragile layer of fur over a form several times larger than the actual finished hat will be. This fragile layer of fur is then carefully wrapped in burlap cloths and immersed for a short time in hot water. The hot water shrinks the fibers slightly—just enough to knit them into a flimsy layer of cloth. This process of shrinking the hood is repeated until it is no bigger than the finished hat and is so tightly felted that a strong man cannot pull it apart. The hat is roughly shaped by wetting and stretching it over a wooden block. The blocks are made from American poplar trees because they have no grain or hard/soft streaks to become imprinted on the felt. A rough shape is obtained by stretching; the finished shape is achieved by blocking the crown and flanging the brim.

Crown stretching is done on a machine. The hood is placed over a frame, with metal fingers above the hood. The fingers "massage" the tip of the cone, pressing the felt between the ribs of the frame, thereby stretching it. The brim stretcher grips the brim with metal fingers and works on the same principle.

Once the taper and crown creases have been created

and a ninety-degree angle has been achieved for the brim, it is then set, or "flanged." First the brim is ironed flat and cut to the specified width. Then it is curled and laid on a wooden flange of desired roll, ironed again, and finally dried and pressed while still on the flange.

At this point, when making a custom hat, personalized fitting begins. The hatmaker takes into consideration not only the wearer's preferences as far as crown height, brim width, etc., but also the individual's physical build. Height and weight will play a part in creating the perfect custom hat with perfect fit, and the experienced professional will take pains to make the hat proportionate to the face and body of the wearer.

Let's take a moment to discuss the varieties of head shapes and sizes, and the proper methods of measuring for a custom hat. Each head has its own size and particular shape, and beyond the fit of the hat, the overall appearance of the hat must conform with the body shape and type of the wearer. A hat may fit perfectly, but if its form, width, height, and breadth do not harmonize with the shape of the customer's skull and face, the end result will not satisfy the wearer. From the outset of the custom hat-

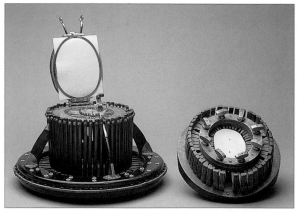

Conformateur, developed in France for precise headwear fitting to any head. (Courtesy of Ritch Rand.)

making process, skull form and size must be a fundamental consideration for the wearer and the hatmaker.

Head size is based on the circumference of the head. If a string is placed around the head and it measures 21.875 inches, and the circumference of the odd oval is made into a circle, the diameter of the circle

LEFT: *Hatter making fur "cones" during hatmaking process.*
(Courtesy of Ritch Rand.)

BELOW: *Some hats can take a shape more closely related to a basic hat "shell" (a hat in process) than a finished hat.*
(Courtesy of Gregory Peterson.)

LEFT: *Chief of Scouts for the U.S. Army during the last Apache campaign in 1885-86, Al Seiber shows off his buckskin outfit, sixgun, and 1886 Winchester carbine.*
(Courtesy of Phil Spangenberger Collection.)

RIGHT: *Hatter inspecting dry "cones," ready for forming into hats.*
(Courtesy of Ritch Rand.)

ABOVE: *This gal was one of the Miller Brothers 101 Ranch Wild West Show riders. She totes a Colt Bisley revolver in her holster and is wearing a split riding skirt typical of the cowgirls at the turn of the century.*
(Courtesy of Phil Spangenberger Collection.)

RIGHT: *Hat styles can become as famous as their owners–here's cowboy poet Waddie Mitchell and his signature crease. Note the "bound edge" (the edge of the hat brim is trimmed with sewn-on binding).*
(Courtesy of Greg Peterson.)

BELOW: *Mixed felt ready for "coning."*

would be 7 inches—the equivalent of a size 7. International hat sizes differ slightly—English sizes are based on the true diameter of a circle, while American sizes deviate slightly. French, Italian, and others using the metric measure have a centimeter (.3927 inch) between sizes, while American and English sizes use the same centimeter differential between sizes.

With the partially constructed hat on your head, the following details should be considered: Is your head shape a round oval or a long oval? How far does the hat come down on your forehead? Is there pressure on the forehead or on the back or sides? Are there flat spots around the band? How wide should the brim be? What about brim edging?

Necessary adjustments are made to the fit by steaming and stretching or pressing the felt hood, and then the finishing process begins. The hat is sanded (yes, with sandpaper!) by hand or by machine, and depending on the desired quality of the finished hat, it is shaved or "pounced" once or several times and "greased" to give a smoother or shinier finish to the felt.

Brim Edging

The edging of a hat brim can be handled in several ways. It may be left plain, known as a "raw edge," or it may be welted or bound with ribbon. Additionally, the folded edge, or "pencil roll," may be used, in which the oversized brim is doubled back and turned into the crown. Pressed and ironed, it forms a soft plump edge and a double brim.

The bound-edge hat brim provides extra tension on the brim, which enables it to hold its snap and keep the brim edge even without buckling or rippling. Additionally, the binding serves to dress up the hat. As in the case of the hatband, the binding color and width can influence the general effect of the hat. A wide binding tends to make the brim look narrower than it actually is. Wide bindings also mean added expense, as more care must be given to prevent wrinkling. And, as you would expect, narrow bindings give the brim a wider look. Binding color also has an impact on the overall look of the hat, as a light-contrast binding on a dark hat will make the hat look lighter. Likewise, a neutral binding on a bright hat will tone it down, and a lighter, brighter-

ABOVE: *Hatter dyes fur to desired color. Natural fur tends to be light brown in color.*
(Courtesy of Ritch Rand.)

color binding on a neutral body will emphasize the color of the hat.

There are three types of ribbon binding on hats. The binding may be the same width on the top and bottom of the brim or may be narrower either on the top or bottom. Several types of stitching are regularly used to attach the binding to the brim: one is the regular, or "through" stitch, which is visible on both sides of the brim; another is the concealed stitch used on homburgs, so that no stitching is visible on the outer side of the rolled brim. There is also the purely ornamental stitch, such as the saddle stitch, and finally, the genuine hand-sewn binding, which is a tedious and painstaking job used on relatively few hats. With this technique, a talented hatmaker can trim only two or three dozen hats per day.

Like ribbon bindings, a welt edge on a hat brim imparts firmness to the edge and helps it hold its shape better and longer, reducing the risk of damage to the shape by the daily handling most hats are subject to. Simply put, the welt edge is a part of the brim that has been folded on itself (either under or over the brim—"under welt" or "over welt") and fixed to stay in place. There are many types of welts, but all are formed by approximately the same production steps. First, the hat brim is curled; then a zinc plate of the proper dimensions is laid on the brim and the curled edge is turned back and ironed flat over the upper side of the plate. The welt is then stitched down, and any excess fur extending beyond the stitching is cut off.

This welting process also adds to the cost of the hat, but such costs can be avoided by choosing a raw-edge brim. The most common raw-edge style is a

Wind and hats don't mix. Armed with this truth, wearers of cowboy hats have created a variety of cord and string methods to keep their hats on, even in the toughest and windiest conditions. These cords or drawstrings have, over the years, been embellished with a variety of materials. Rawhide, latigo leather, and horsehair have all been utilized as fashion add-ons in making these cords more attractive and individual to the style of the wearer. The name "stampede string" has come to describe these cords as an obvious result of application—it'll keep your hat on even in the middle of a cattle stampede—a uniquely western solution!

straight edge, but for a bit of flair, the edge of the brim can be slanted or rounded, which also lends strength to the brim.

The finest and most expensive hats have a hand-felted edge, in which the edge is formed into the brim edge as an integral part of the hat, and therefore requires no stitching. Ordinarily, fur shrinks too fast and unevenly for the purpose of creating a hand-felted edge, but it looks better and lasts longer than any other welt, even though it requires more time and effort to create. Hats with hand-felted edges require constant individual supervision from beginning to end of fabrication and shaping.

Sweatbands

After sanding, the sweatband is installed, a process that requires great precision. There can be no lumps or irregular lines to the sweatband; it cannot leave red marks on the customer's forehead; it should grip the customer's head just tightly enough so that the hat will stay on in a mild to medium breeze; and the band itself cannot be too thick or it will distort the set and shape of the brim and crown.

The quality of the leather for the sweatband is also a very important factor. Because it is the only part of the completed hat that touches the head, it is imperative that the leather be soft, well-fitted, and absorbent, or the wearer will never fully enjoy the hat. Most hat leathers are made from sheepskin and lambskin. These skins are imported to the United States from other countries around the world, with the majority coming from Argentina and New Zealand.

Sheepskin and lambskin are used for hat leathers because they have the requisite properties. They are open textured and easily absorb perspiration. In addition, they are neither too soft, too stiff, nor too porous. Calfskin also makes a fine hat leather, but its high cost generally limits its use. Synthetic leathers are frequently used in lower-priced hats, and thanks to the modern synthetics manufactured today, these synthetic leathers can provide the wearer with many of the qualities of leather for a much lower price. Occasionally, grosgrain ribbon or other fabric is used for sweatbands where extreme light weight and flexibility are a factor.

Hat leathers come in two types—roans and skivers. The roan is the whole skin with none of the flesh side shaved off. Skiver leathers have been split in two, with only the outer or grain side being used to make the sweatband. Roans, with their plumpness and tensile strength, go into the better hats. Skivers are usually used in medium- and lower-grade hats, or where light weight is a primary concern. More than twenty-five different operations are necessary to transform raw skins into the finished product.

Once the sweatband has been cut, shaped, and dyed, the two ends are then sewn together and a small fabric bow is attached by hand at the top of the joint. The sweatband is then carefully machine-stitched into the hat.

This brings us to the mystery of the sweatband ribbon. Just about everyone has wondered, at one time or another, what the little ribbon bow at the back of the sweatband is for. We've done some extensive research on this issue, and have heard several different interpretations. At one time, the author considered it to be some sort of size adjustment aid, and indeed, in the eighteenth century, hats were made one-size-fits-all. Each hat was constructed with a ribbon running through the sweatband to be tied with a bow at the back, allowing the sweatband to be tightened or loosened as needed. Presumably, the bow we see today is merely a nod at tradition. We've also heard that the bow is no more than a subtle reference to where the back of the hat is, thus helping the wearer avoid the embarrassment of putting his hat on backwards. Yet another theory claims that the bow is a measurement guide for the hatter, precisely locating the center of the back, which the hatter uses to create a straight crease in the hat's crown.

By far the most interesting and inventive story regarding the origin of the bow claims that it is actually a stylized danger symbol. It seems that in the hatting industry, around the turn of the century, hatters used small amounts of mercury in the felting process. Mercury poisoning has the same symptoms as Alzheimer's disease, and hatters who were exposed to mercury for an extended period of time would begin to show these symptoms—hence the origin of the term "mad hatter." The hatting industry needed to come to terms with the fact that there was a potential toxin in the felt of the hat, and the little bow on the sweatband was a stylized version of the

LEFT: *Hats being finished in finishing department. Brims are being sanded to a smooth finish. Circa 1930s.* (Courtesy of Bailey Hats.)

LOWER LEFT: *Every little girl dreams of being a rodeo queen and putting on a "Cowgirl Crown."* (Courtesy of Gregory Peterson.)

LOWER RIGHT: *Becoming a hat is not easy; note the rope on these flattening rollers. Ouch!* (Courtesy of Ritch Rand.)

skull and crossbones, warning the buyer that there was a toxic material within the fur.

Sometimes, in the modern-day sweatband, the leather is reeded for added appearance and comfort. Originally, rattan reeds were used in this process, but in today's hat market a resilient synthetic thread is encased in hatter's glaze and, together with an oiled-silk insert, is sewn to the leather at the base of the brim. Reeded leathers are plumper looking and they cushion the head better, and the oiled-silk insert underneath is added protection against perspiration staining the felt. However, reeded leathers necessarily add to the cost of the hat.

There are also foam sweatbands on the market, consisting of a bond of plastic or rubber foam, with fabric facing laminated on the side next to the head. It provides a yielding, cushioned fit and can overcome slight variations in head size. Additionally, there are stretch sweatbands made of new stretch fibers, which spring back to softly cling to the head for the life of the hat. These stretch sweatbands make it easy to fit the between-size head in non-custom hats.

After the sweatband has been carefully sewn into the hood, it is turned in and the threads of the sweatband are smoothed down to prevent them from leaving imprints on the wearer's forehead.

Finishes

Expert hatmakers finish their hats in one of several ways. These finishes add to the final beauty of a well-made hat. The silk finish, the most luxurious, is a long-fur finish with a characteristic sheen of silk. It is created by either buffing the long nap with a felt wheel, or by smoothing the nap with a special pad and grease. Similar to the luxurious look and feel of the silk finish, the angora finish is another long-hair style. Oddly enough, no angora hair is used to create the hat—the term refers only to the luxurious, furry feel and look of the finished hat. It is fashioned by leaving the fur long throughout the entire hatmaking process, and using a long wire brush for scratching the long fur in the finishing process.

The beaver finish does not concern itself with the amount of (or lack of) beaver fur in the felt. Rather, it refers to a hat in which the nap is left long and combed out horizontally. Made from long, selected fur, it has a long, dense nap and a beautiful luster, which is emphasized when buffed with a buffing wheel. It differs from the silk finish in that the beaver finish consists of longer fur and a shorter nap.

The velour finish is famous for its deep, lustrous nap, like that of fine velvet. Of all the finishes, the velour finish is the most pleasing to the touch. To create this look and feel, the hat body is "sharkskinned," meaning that the nap is combed up and the short fur fibers are pulled out with real sharkskin strips mounted on a rapidly spinning wheel. Then the fur fibers are clipped to an even length.

A suede finish on a hat is sometimes referred to as the "antelope" or "doe" finish. It can be distinguished from the regular smooth-finish felt by a slightly discernible sheen, where the light catches the ends of the fur, and by its soft, velvetlike surface. To achieve this finish, the hat is buffed with emery paper, which abrades the fur to the desired height, and then polished with the felt wheel, which not only adds luster but brings up the nap.

A sponge finish, also known as the "chinchilla" or "pebble" finish, is distinguished by the many tiny knobs or clumps of fur covering the entire surface of the hat, giving it a nubby appearance. This finish is perfect when worn with strongly textured clothes such as rough tweeds. The knobs are produced in the fur by moistening the surface and then rubbing it in an elliptical motion.

STETSON

A scratch finish can be used on any type of felt, and is accomplished by scratching the surface of the fur with a wire brush in the final stages of production. This process loosens up the surface hairs, leaving them rough and hairy, or they can be laid into a long, smooth nap with further brushing. Scratch finishes can be produced in long, medium, or short finish.

Linings

Linings of good hats were originally made of fine satins. With the improvement of synthetic textiles, most linings today are made of rayon, with two principal types of rayon linings in use: satin rayon, which has a smooth surface, a lustrous face, and a dull back; and taffeta rayon, which is a fine, plain-weave fabric, smooth on both sides, without the high luster of satin. Because taffeta is generally a lighter fabric than satin, it is used in lighter-weight hats.

We've heard the question again and again: What makes the lining stay in? Since most linings in even the finest hats are sewn only at the bottom edge, it's not a silly question. The fact is that linings are exactly tailored to each hat, and the inserting is done by skilled workers. Careless or inept work can spoil the interior appearance of the hat, and lining application can be a very telling indicator as to the overall care and skill that went into the making of a particular hat.

For the best grade of hat, individual linings are made not only for each head size, but also for each crown height. For other hats, one lining can be substituted in a hat with a different crown height. This can be done if they do not differ by more than one-fourth of an inch. The sweatband will conceal any difference, but in a well-done assembly, the seam in the lining should line up with the joint in the sweatband and with the center of the dye in the tip.

Hatbands

After the lining is put in, a selfband or outer hatband is then applied. The felt for the selfband is taken from the brim or other section of the original crown felt to ensure that it matches perfectly. The selfband is cut, finished, and then affixed to the outer portion of the hat with a buckle or concho to prevent it from coming off.

For every hat there is a band; it is merely up to the wearer to choose one. Luckily, the "urban cowboy" day is past, and with it, the era of the two-inch feather band.

CENTER: *Hat linings are elegant identity statements by hatters and are some of the finest examples of label art. The woven "Last Drop From His Stetson" logo/lining is an icon of the American West.* (Courtesy of Hat Brands Inc.)

BOTTOM: *Hat trims add a truly personal touch to any hat. They come in an infinite variety of styles from the simple self-banding cut from the brim of the hat, to horsehair, to beaded, to silver—the options are limitless.* (Courtesy of Az-Tex Hats Co. And Montana Silversmith.)

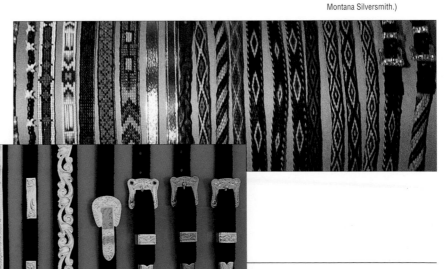

Taking Care of a Cowboy Hat

Sure, you polish your boots before you go out on the town; sure, you polish your car before taking it out and showing it off; but did you know that you should regularly shine up your cowboy hat as well? Yep, and here's a surprise—you might even get yourself some sandpaper and rub 'er down now and again, too.

Most western hats come in black or pastel shades—silver belly, cream, bleached, or natural beaver—and they look so sharp and fresh when you first walk out of the hatter's! But no matter how careful the wearer is, the hat soon becomes discolored with smudges, smears, oil stains, and sweat stains. Supposedly clean hands deposit dirt and damaging oils, which soil the felt every time they touch it. Dust flies everywhere—indoors and out (if you don't think so, try wiping your hat with a clean handkerchief and see what you end up with).

Rather than taking your soiled hat to a hat-factory facility for an expensive, professional renovation and cleaning, you can keep your nice new hat in tip-top condition with regular touch-ups done at home with minimal time, energy, and cost. A properly kept, $25 hat can look a lot better than a $250 beaver that's covered with smudges, grime, and dust.

Dust to Dust

Regular dusting is the first, easiest, and most important hat-tending duty. Use only a soft-bristled brush for the daily removal of dust. Many western stores use and sell hatter's brushes made for this purpose. A black brush for the darker hats and a light one for the pastel colors keeps both types cleaner than trying to use one brush for all colors. Avoid whisk-type brooms as they have far too rough a bristle and will tear the fine surface of fur felt. All types of brushes will remove surface dirt only; they will not eliminate deeper smudges or oily finger marks.

Another way to accomplish regular dust removal is by wiping the hat with a damp bath towel. A Turkish towel, moistened from drying off after a shower, does a fine job of removing dust—no need to moisten it further. Your standard terry-cloth bath towels have a slight nap—not enough to damage the fur—and can be used rather briskly to remove dust without fear of damaging or distorting the hat's surface or shape. And here's the key: Always rub in a circular, counterclockwise motion. Rubbing a hat clockwise is

like trying to stroke a cat from tail to head—it isn't satisfying for the hat or the wearer!

Ex-Sponge Those Stains

When stains are too deep to remove by brushing or rubbing the hat, try using a soft, small-pored rubber sponge, such as a woman's makeup sponge or a small piece of foam rubber. Rubber sponges have a slight "tack" that grabs the outer layer of the felt and pulls out the soiled materials. Any kind of sponge acts like an art-gum eraser by removing surface soiling as you would remove pencil marks from a sketch. In fact, an art-gum eraser can also be used for the same purpose, so long as you rub in a counterclockwise direction with the grain.

Gotta Be Rough to Be Smooth

For the marks that sponging will not remove, sanding is the next step to take. Use only the finest grit sandpaper for this process such as you would use for the final finish to a piece of fine-grained wooden furniture. Moving the sandpaper in a counter-clockwise motion, very gently and cautiously touch the dirty surface. Never dig in, and never put your finger inside the hat to push outward against the sandpaper! This forces the sandpaper into the felt, cutting too deeply and creating a thin, weak spot. In most cases where sandpapering is required, remove no more felt than your skin loses when it peels after a sunburn, if that much.

Oil's Well That Ends Well

Is your hat permanently stained if you get a dab of butter or a smear of oil on it? Not necessarily. For accidents like this, where the stain has not penetrated too deeply, you can try another home remedy in the form of a product called Fuller's Earth. Drug or paint stores sell Fuller's Earth in small containers; it has the fine consistency of baking

ABOVE: *This cowgirl has to take special care of her hat with an edge bound with hand beading. A true piece of cowboy/girl hat art.*
(Courtesy of Gregory Peterson.)

FAR LEFT: *No need to give up on a good hat just because it's seen a little wear.*
(Courtesy of Gregory Peterson.)

powder with a taupe or tan color. Do not concern yourself with the color of the powder; it will not stain your hat. After brushing off the hat, simply sprinkle the Fuller's Earth on and around the spot to a depth of about one-eighth of an inch.

Like a poultice that draws an infection from a sore on your horse, this little poultice of Fuller's Earth draws the oily residue from the fibers in your hat. Let the poultice sit for two or three hours, and then brush it off with a soft brush or towel. If a sign of the spot remains, shake on another poultice and allow it to stand for another few hours. Carefully brush away the powder on the surface, and then work out the

professional renovator, who will restore your pride and joy to its former beauty. Generally, hats with heavy sweat stains must be taken to a professional, as they run far deeper than the surface of the felt. Once the professional renovator has done his job, it's up to you to keep the hat sharp and clean with regular brushing! We can't emphasize this enough; it makes an enormous difference in the look and life of your hat.

BELOW: *Circa late 1860s or early 1870s, this photo shows what appears to be a genuine, punchy-type cowboy, complete with "ironed" flat brim hat.* (Courtesy of Phil Spangenberger Collection.)

Pick It Up, Put It Down

Daily dirt and grime are not the only enemies of a nice felt hat. The manner in which the hat is handled has a lot to do with its longevity. First and foremost, avoid touching your hat if your hands are dirty or oily—this is the one thing that will cut the life and looks of a nice hat down to nothing. When you do pick up your hat, don't do so by grabbing the brim, as the weight of the rest of the hat will weaken the set or angle of the brim, be it flat or curved. Picking the hat up by both front and back brims is preferable. The best way to pick up a hat is, of course, from beneath. If the hat is

remaining powder that has penetrated the felt, using the plastic or rubber sponge. Remember to rub counterclockwise!

When the oily stain on your hat is so deep that none of these remedies are successful, we suggest you take your hat to a

on a hat stand, hook, or block, this is done quite easily and puts the least stress on the brim, crown, etc.

Never, never rest the hat flat on a flat surface, particularly if the hat has a snap brim. To preserve the scope, or pitch, of the hat brim, the downward-bending front part should always hang over the edge of its resting surface. Thrown carelessly on a table, the hat's brim will curl upward, front and back, drawing the sides down and ruining the brim shape. Another way to put the hat down is to rest it upside down on its crown; however, be careful to put it on a clean surface. A last word of warning—don't let the

ABOVE: *An unusual shot of a hat not on someone's head—the true westerner would never park his hat while daylight burned. The pinch-front crease is known today as a Tom Horn crease after the famous cattle detective.*
(Courtesy of Gregory Peterson.)

ABOVE: *This pair of hombres both sport one of the most often-worn styles of headgear in the Old West: the flat-brimmed, straight-sided crown with rounded corners. This popular hat was known as the "Boss of the Plains" style and was sold by just about every hatter throughout the U.S. While these hats are most likely Stetsons, the style was made by several firms, and was popular from well before the Civil War until long after the turn of the century. This is the style of hat that was adopted by the U.S. Forest Service (with added "Montana" or "Smokey the Bear" creased crown). This type of hat is often seen in C. M. Russell paintings and has continued in popularity as shown (at far left) on veteran western actor Gary Cooper. (Courtesy of Ritch Rand.)*

RIGHT: *Randolph Scott, redefining a fedora-style crease.*
(Courtesy of Ritch Rand.)

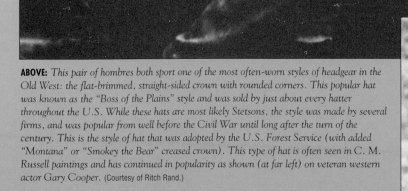

clerk at the hatcheck counter stack your hat on top of (or underneath) other hats. This type of stacking can stretch or buckle your crown and brim—a problem that requires a professional hat blocker to properly resize (if it can be done at all).

At Day's End

Turning out the leather sweatband after a perspiring day preserves the life of any hat. With the leather turned out, perspiration and hair oil evaporate and dry out instead of soaking into the hat. (This also applies to straw hats.) If a hat gets rain-soaked, put out the creases and dents, get it as even and round as possible, and if the brim is turned down, turn it up again. Turn out the leather, stand the hat on the leather on a clean, level surface, and leave it there until it dries naturally. Do not use artificial heat. Pressure of any sort on the soaking-wet hat will leave its mark when the hat dries. Don't jam the brim against anything or it will buckle while drying and will stay that way. Once the hat has dried, you can recreate the creases with a little careful measurement and a gentle hand.

ABOVE LEFT: *Frank Hamer (standing, left) with other Texas Rangers, photographed in Del Rio, Texas. Rangers were, as a group, perceived as larger than life, and their approach to headwear reflected this.*
(Courtesy of Phil Spangenberger Collection.)

FAR RIGHT: *This contemporary photo (1990s) shows the reverence returning not only for older hat styles, but also for early western apparel.*
(Courtesy of Gregory Peterson.)

LEFT: *This Durango, Colorado, silver miner, circa early 1870s sports the nineteenth century classic bib-front shirt with embroidered-edged bib. His high-waisted trousers are held up by a natural fit. A close look at the photo reveals a suspender button on the waistband. His wide-brimmed hat is turned up in front in typical western fashion, and the square-toed boots feature the paneled fronts on the top. His carbine is the Model 1860 Spencer in .56-56 cal.*
(Courtesy of Phil Spangenberger Collection.)

RIGHT: *Broad-brimmed, low crown hats were often favored in the early West as shown by this pair of young, Pueblo, Colorado, hunters. The man at left sports an 1186 Model Winchester and a Colt Single Action at his hip. His hat is adorned with a leather band and probably brass or nickeled harness spots attached. His shotgun-wielding pard also wears a Colt Peacemaker at his side and his flat-brimmed "conk cover," as westerners sometimes called their hats, is fitted with a braided double leather band.*
(Courtesy of Phil Spangenberger Collection.)

Bailey Hats

ABOVE: *Bailey's signature Clint Black ad and hat (at right).*

ABOVE RIGHT: *An early shot of the Bailey factory.* (Courtesy of Bailey Hat Co.)

RIGHT: *The classic Mesquite-style hat shown here features a "Cattleman" crease and "Longhorn" brim flange shape. Bailey hats feature a patented sweatband with a "Cushion Ride" comfort feature.* (Courtesy of Bailey Hat Co.)

In 1922, George S. Bailey started in the hat business. His young son, Chuck Bailey, who would later run the family business, worked in the factory as a schoolboy. Chuck sold the company and later retired in 1994. Today the Bailey Hat Company is one of the largest makers of western hats in the world.

Bailey straw hats were the first to have a wire in the brim for easy shaping. These "U-Rollit" straws set the standard in design for all straw hats to follow.

Bailey Hats are made in Texas and Pennsylvania and are worn by rodeo and working cowboys alike.

The company also manufactures a line of casual hat styles as well as its many styles of felt and straw western hats.

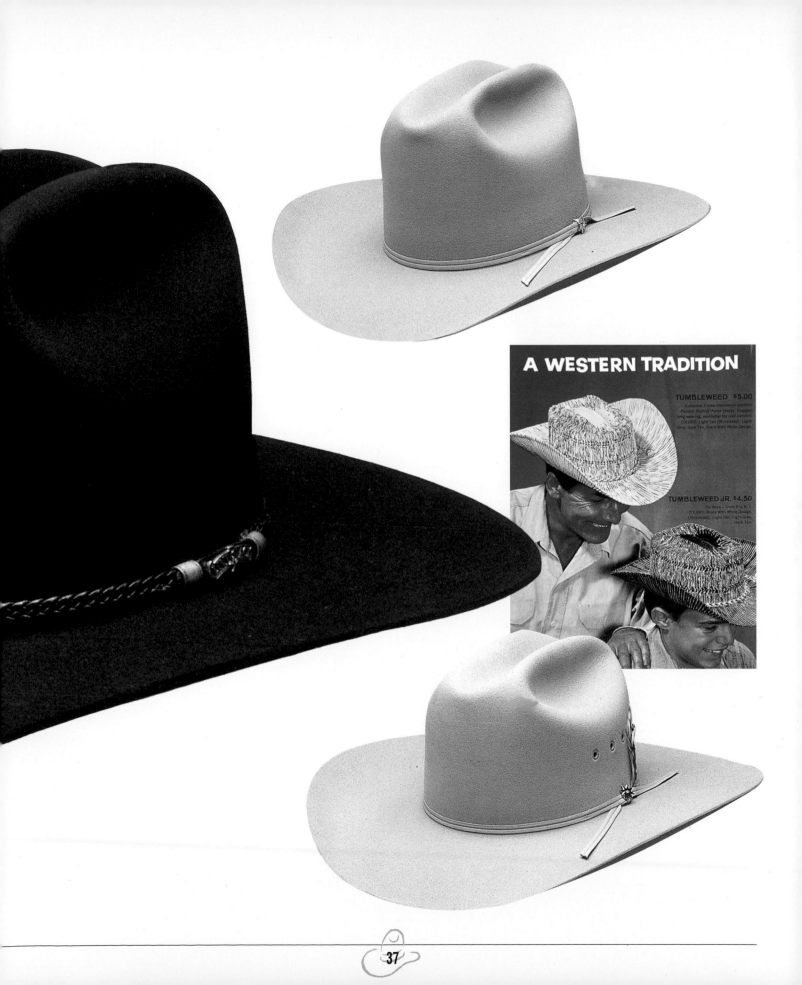

A WESTERN TRADITION

TUMBLEWEED $5.00

Exclusive 2-tone interweave pattern. Popular Roping Horse theme. Rugged, long wearing, ventilated for cool comfort. COLORS: Light Tan (Illustrated), Light Grey, Dark Tan, Black with White Design

TUMBLEWEED JR. $4.50

For boys – Sizes 6¼ to 7. COLORS: Black with White Design (Illustrated), Light Tan, Light Grey, Dark Tan.

Resistol Hats

Best All-Around ...again.

Ty Murray
6 Time World All-Around Champion

WHEN YOU'RE GOOD, YOU'RE GOOD, BUT WHEN YOU'RE GREAT, YOU CAN BE CHAMPION. AT THE 1994 NFR, TY MURRAY JOINED THE RANKS OF RODEO LEGENDS TOM FERGUSON AND LARRY MAHAN, THE ONLY PRCA COMPETITORS EVER TO WIN SIX WORLD ALL-AROUND CHAMPION TITLES. WE AT RESISTOL ARE PROUD TO RIDE WITH TY MURRAY, WORLD ALL-AROUND CHAMPION, AGAIN.

RESISTOL

ABOVE: *A current Resistol ad image features rodeo legend Ty Murray. Resistol is considered the working cowboy's hat.*
(Courtesy of Hat Brands Inc.)

In the early 1920s young millionaire E. R. Byer sold his business in Michigan and traveled south to further his fortune and investment. His investment was a brilliant young hatmaker, Harry Rolnick, who was operating a small hat factory. E. R. Byer was one of Rolnick's customers and was so impressed by Harry's professionalism, flair for fashion, and devotion to quality that in 1927 the firm of Byer-Rolnick was founded in Dallas, Texas. The company produced men's felt hats in western and dress stylings. Both were marketed under the newly created name "Resistol Hats," meaning to resist all weather.

Distribution was limited to Texas and Oklahoma early on, but innovations like the Self-Conforming Band® and Kitten Finish® (an innovation in the finishing process of felt) gained national exposure and in 1938 prompted expansion to a larger facility in Garland, Texas, where Resistol hats are manufactured today.

Byer-Rolnick's success continued, and the Resistol brand became the greatest name in western hats. In an effort to better control the quality and flow of its product, Byer-Rolnick acquired a fur-cutting plant

CENTER: *The classic 20X "Black Gold" de rigueur for rodeo. Other styles shown are the popular "Ambush" (above) and the "Hill Country" (below).*
(Courtesy of Hat Brands Inc.)

and built a rough body plant in Longview, Texas. These acquisitions made Byer-Rolnick the first and only manufacturer to operate the entire felt hatmaking process, which includes over 200 steps. By operating all phases of production, Byer-Rolnick was able to obtain maximum quality control and thereby produce the most consistent and finest hat known the world over.

Demand for Resistol hats continued, and today "the small hat factory" is part of Arena Brands, Inc., the largest manufacturer of headwear in the world. All phases of production are still operated and controlled to ensure a product of the highest quality.

Stetson Hats

Buffalo Bill Cody

It's a
STETSON

In 1865, with $100, John B. Stetson rented a small room, bought the tools he needed, bought $10 worth of fur, and the John B. Stetson Hat Company was born. A year later, the "Hat of the West," or the now-famous "Boss of the Plains" hat, was born, and the name Stetson was on its way to becoming the mark of quality, durability, innovation, and beauty.

John B. Stetson experienced trying times in his life, but after it all he relied on the one thing he did exceptionally well, making hats. He was trained by his father, a master hatter, and applied his skills and knowledge to a trade that, at the time, was not held in high regard.

A hatter was seen as unreliable, lazy or aloof, only looking to make his money and go have fun. John B. Stetson changed all that and built one of America's most successful businesses. The longevity and history of the John B. Stetson Company is based on innovations and quality! John B. Stetson led the hat industry his entire career by designing new hat styles for fashion and function. Quality was his creed and has been for the past 130 years—so much so that the word and the name Stetson are synonymous.

Today the Stetson hat factory in St. Joseph, Missouri, is one of the largest in the country and produces a line of hats in hundreds of different styles and colors. In spite of this company's size, however, classic styling and premium quality remain as the driving forces behind each and every hat. As a result, Stetson hats are the best-known hats in the world. Wherever and whenever hats are discussed, Stetson will be mentioned.

Charlie 1 Horse

ABOVE:
Recognized quite easily by the firebrand mark on the crown as a Charlie 1 Horse hat, The Limited Edition 30X beaver features a 14K solid-gold logo and diamonds and comes with a signature hat case.
(Courtesy of Hat Brands Inc.)

Founded in 1980, Charlie 1 Horse is a manufacturer of a unique line of custom-designed western hats. The now-famous, front-decorated western hats and the genuine firebrand are unmistakably Charlie. The introduction of Charlie 1 Horse and its early success was based on very specialized styles with limited availability. This strategy made the brand a sought-after exclusive.

Charles 1 Horse's continued success is based on superior service, quality product, and a customized approach to hat trimming and finishing. Charlie 1 Horse served a targeted niche within the western-hat market by offering premium-priced, uniquely designed hats that spoke to the individualistic western consumer. Today this niche is referred to as "Designer Western," and Charlie 1 Horse remains its sole occupant.

While the designer western niche is Charlie 1 Horse's core, the line has broadened over the years to offer other premium lines that include traditional western styles, Wild West styles, and the Custom Triple XXX Fur Blend Collection, and provide designer western styles at popular price points.

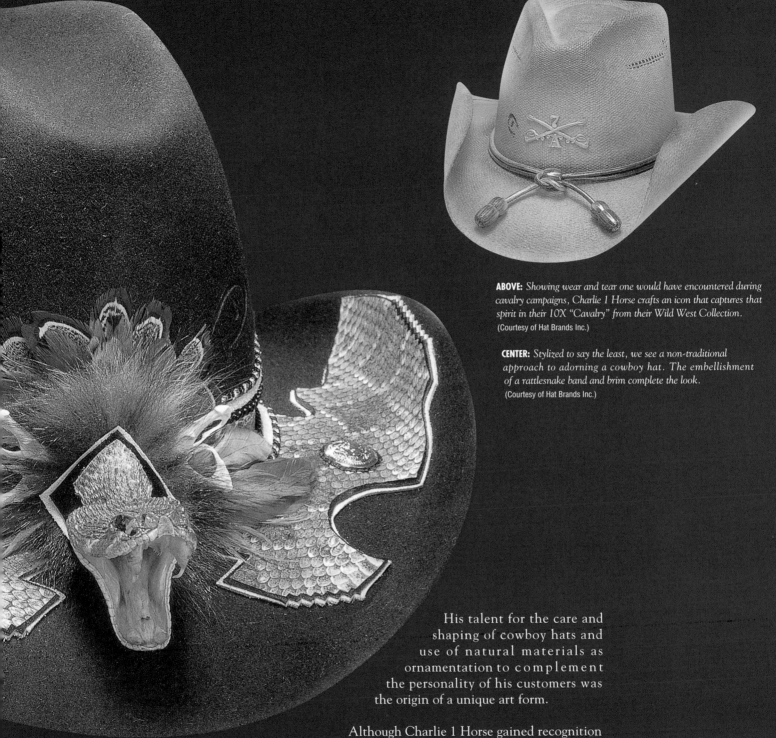

ABOVE: *Showing wear and tear one would have encountered during cavalry campaigns, Charlie 1 Horse crafts an icon that captures that spirit in their 10X "Cavalry" from their Wild West Collection.* (Courtesy of Hat Brands Inc.)

CENTER: *Stylized to say the least, we see a non-traditional approach to adorning a cowboy hat. The embellishment of a rattlesnake band and brim complete the look.* (Courtesy of Hat Brands Inc.)

His talent for the care and shaping of cowboy hats and use of natural materials as ornamentation to complement the personality of his customers was the origin of a unique art form.

Although Charlie 1 Horse gained recognition for his work in the mountains outside of Taos, New Mexico, his reputation spread over the midwest and western states. Fortunately, his skills and knowledge have been passed on to the equally skilled artisans who make Charlie 1 Horse hats today.

The talent for trimming a hat with natural band materials dates back to the days of the Old West and the legend of the Indian Charlie 1 Horse. Charlie 1 Horse earned his reputation for restoring pride to worn-out hats.

The Montecristi Custom Hat Works

Milton Johnson, custom hatter.

For over 25 years Milton Johnson has directed the crafting of fine Panama straw and fur felt hats at Santa Fe's Montecristi Custom Hat Works. Recognized as one of the world's finest makers of straw hats, Johnson also specializes in fine hand-finished fur hats with exceptional bandings. While at home working with the many celebrity customers he has, such as Tom Selleck, Sam Elliott and Lucas Black to name a few, Johnson says his real satisfaction is the sight of a "crooked smile" breaking out across the weathered face of a working cowboy who has just settled into his new Montecristi. That, he says, is the real reward for a hard-working custom hatter.

The "Buckaroo" and the "Derby"—one classic, one contemporary.
(Courtesy Montecristi Custom Hat Works.)

BELOW: *500X Beaver /
Chinchilla hat with 18kt
gold Jim Neely hatband.*
(Courtesy of Montecristi Custom
Hat Works.)

Rand's Hats

ABOVE: *Veteran hatter Ritch Rand.*
(Courtesy of Rand's Hats.)

A Rand's custom hat is recognized as an example of uncompromising dedication to quality. Using the finest furs and felts, each hat is completely handmade following the age-old methods used by fine hatmakers a century ago. Ritch Rand started in the hat business over twenty years ago as an apprentice to an elderly master hatter. His long and detailed training resulted in Ritch's strong belief in the traditional methods of hatmaking and a true dedication to quality. Rand's line of hats include the only officially approved Charlie Russell Hat (approved by the Charlie Russell Museum in Great Falls, Montana), which is an exact replica of Russell's recognizable hat.

Here's the true Old West look in the Tom Horn style, with a 4" brim and 6" crown, shown in distressed finish. Distressing adds an authentic look to an early west design.
(Courtesy of Ritch Rand.)

Rand's Custom Hats are diverse in their design. Pictured here are classic Rand's hats including the Charles M. Russell hat that Ritch crafted for the Russell Museum in Great Falls, Montana. Below is one of Ritch's "distressed" hats.
(Courtesy of Ritch Rand.)

Michael Malone

He was born in Texas and raised in the panhandle ranching country around Amarillo, absorbing the horse traditions of the high plains.

He has been an artist and craftsman all his life, playing stringed instruments since the first grade. He studied watercolor, printmaking, and painting in New Mexico, where he lived until 1975. Upon returning to Texas, he pursued music and leather design while applying his knowledge of cowboy gear to making and designing western hats in Austin and Fort Worth. Mr. Malone's teachers were Manny Gammage, Whistle Ryon, and the seat of his britches.

Through the years, his connections with musicians and horse and cow people kept him doing designs for Emmylou Harris, Ian Tyson, Jerry Jeff Walker, Michael Martin Murphey, and Peter Newman, as well as working for such diverse personalities as Little Feat, Lyle Lovett,

ABOVE, LEFT and BELOW:
Malone works magic with his hats in creating one-of-a-kind western headwear. Cutouts, inlays, and lacing are part of Michael Malone's palette as he hand-works his hats into unique statements of the American West.
(Courtesy of M. Malone.)

and the Rolling Stones. He also did work for movie and television projects.

His interest in historical authenticity is his biggest influence. So, his hat designs reflect the older-style California influences of the vaquero, as well as the Taos/Santa Fe mountain-man look. He has been hand painting sweat-stained hats since the early eighties for movies, and that look is surprisingly popular, along with the edge-laced and leather filigree hats Mr. Malone features at shows and exhibits.

Buying Your First Hat — A Survival Guide

(or All I Ever Needed To Know I Learned From A Cowboy Hat Salesman)

The late cowboy character actor Dub Taylor being fitted by a youthful Ritch Rand for the perfect fit. Year - unknown, as Ritch wouldn't admit he was that old.
(Courtesy Ritch Rand.)

BACKGROUND: *How not to look in a cowboy hat. Obviously these fellows did not take to heart the suggestions of their local hat sales professional.*
(Courtesy William Reynolds.)

It can be overwhelming. For many the idea of walking into a western store is more than they can take. Do I walk differently? Do I speak like Slim Pickens? Do I cast a faraway glance? No, no, a thousand times, no! The western store experience is not something to be feared. Where that idea came from eludes me, but I digress.

Buying a hat is a conscious decision; rarely is it an impulse purchase, so one must be ready to view oneself with headwear—a vision for many that is tough at first, especially on a good-hair day. It is at this point though, when one is ready to make the move, to make the commitment that one must be prepared to put trust in the seasoned experience of the hat-department sales person. It is this professional's job to make you look good in a hat. So good that you will be literally compelled to wear the hat from the store rather than carry it out in its corrugated container.

A good-fitting hat changes your life. A strong statement? Maybe. But until one goes through the experience it cannot be described adequately. Here's why: The solid, knowledgeable hat salesperson does not want his customer to look like a dork. He loses sales and hurts return business. He knows which hats work best with slim faces, round faces, tall people and short people. His job is to make you walk out of the store feeling like the Duke. If he doesn't, you won't come back, it's that simple.

Wearing a hat makes sense, he'll tell you. It keeps the sun and rain off of you, helps protect you from getting skin cancer, and generally gives one a rather classic and punchy appearance. Ask anyone what a cowboy hat conjures up and you'll hear words like "strength," "individuality," "self-reliance," "honesty," "loyalty" and "humility." How can any of those be bad? What does a ball cap conjure up? Depends on where the bill is placed, right?

RIGHT: *Great hat, great fit, great cowboy star Jim Davis.*
(Courtesy Ritch Rand.)

BELOW/RIGHT: *All hats are not for everyone. Some can wear a derby style while others need a broader brim like this modified "Tom Horn."*
(Courtesy Ritch Rand.)

The movies have been a double-edged sword and may have given the cowboy hat a bad rap. It's been years since John Travolta two-stepped his way into the hearts of non-hat wearers in his *Urban Cowboy* mode, creating a false bubble in hat purchases. A dark period for hatters. Remember, cowboys' hats are not a trend, they are literally a way of life. They help us remember where we came from and why we are as great a nation as we are.

During your hat try-on—and ultimately, purchase—your hat professional will share all of this with you. So think about it. Buying a hat is not just a transaction; it is really a deep look into the origin and basis of this great country. It is a review of values we hold dear, a window on our own legacy, and most of all, an honest retrospective of a great way of life. Besides, hats are cool. Wear yours with pride.

Great Hats, Great Hat People

H ats speak the language of life experience—the experience of being a part of their owner. On the following pages, we have assembled some very unique hats alongside some great hat people. These are just a few of the many out there, but they represent the wide array of diverse and eclectic styles just as the hats and people on this page. From contemporary cowboys to legendary western celebrities and heroes, they're all here.

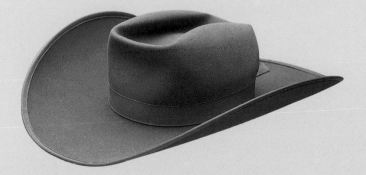

Incredible Green & Purple 1950s Cowgirl Hats
This exceptional, dark green cowgirl hat from the 1950s was made by the Eddy Bros., *Barrel Racer*-style name. The hat above belongs to a stunning ensemble worn by the elegant Martha Satin. Her close and long-time friend Rex Allen commissioned Nudie to custom-make the shirt and pants. Rhinestone studded cream gabardine embroidered with red roses with long green stems and leaves; the green hat was a perfect accent. Mr. Allen gave Martha the entire outfit as a gift in the fifties. The purple hat is similar in design.
(All courtesy of the Gene Autry Western Heritage Museum.)

Hispanic Felt Hat

This black felt hat has an oval-shaped crown with a flat top and a wide (4¼") flat brim. Gold accents decorate the hat, with gold thread lace-like appliqués around the brim, a matching hatband, and a chin strap (drawn through crown grommets) made of tan yarn covered in gold metallic thread.

(Courtesy of the Gene Autry Western Heritage Museum.)

Stetson Custom Hat

Made by the Stetson Company for the California Clothing Company of Los Angeles, and worn by Leo Carrillo, this handsome off-white hat shows off a wide 4½" brim, and bears an imprint in the crown for the California Clothing Company of Los Angeles.

(Courtesy of the Gene Autry Western Heritage Museum.)

Stetson Pressed-Felt Hat

For the pure 1870s look, this grey-green Stetson features a broad flat brim, straight crown with puckers around the edges, air-vent holes around the top of the crown, and a green grosgrain ribbon hatband. The Stetson sticker on the inner crown is printed with a "7." It was owned and worn by "Antelope" Ernst Baumann, a market hunter, army scout, and Denver lawman, active in the 1870s-80s.

(Courtesy of the Gene Autry Western Heritage Museum.)

Nudie's Personal 5X Stetson with Rhinestone Hatband

This gorgeous off-white Stetson was personally used by Nudie himself! A beautiful 5X beaver with a triangular crease and an upturned brim, it is accented with an amazing hatband consisting of silver-colored leather with three rows of rhinestones and a small silver-toned buckle. Nudie's stamp and sticker prices for hat and band appear on the sweatband. Worn by Nudie Cohn in the 1980s.
(Courtesy of the Gene Autry Western Heritage Museum.)

Roy Rogers
No cowboy hat book would be complete without Roy—slicked up in his Bohlin belt buckles.
(Courtesy of Ritch Rand.)

Jack Mahoney
A veteran western character.
(Courtesy of the Phil Spangenberger Collection.)

Fancy Lining Classic Vaquero Hat
This off-white felt hat, with off-white grosgrain ribbon hatband and brim edges, bears the following imprinted notation on the commercial leather sweatband: "Hutchinsons A Mark of Quality Los Angeles." The gorgeous crown lining bears the image of a cowboy watering his horse using his "ten-gallon" hat. This is the classic hat favored by the few working California vaqueros in the 1930s.
(Courtesy of the Gene Autry Western Heritage Museum.)

Yellowstone Kelly *Cavalry Officer's Hat*

This black felt cavalry officer's hat was worn in the film *Yellowstone Kelly* in 1959. The manufacturer's name stamped inside the band reads "Bailey Royal, Made in California." Two rows of tan cord are wrapped around the crown base, passing through a barrel-shaped bead and tied (each cord has a wrapped head). On the front of the crown is a gold-colored metal double-sword emblem, sewed with gold thread.

(Courtesy of the Gene Autry Western Heritage Museum.)

Marie Windsor's Stetson

This off-white Stetson with black hatband, trim, and leather string strap was owned and worn by Marie Windsor when she won a small-town beauty contest in Utah in the 1930s (before she came to Hollywood to begin her acting career). The hat is autographed by other beauty contest participants and numerous actors who took part in the festivities. Windsor went on to act in hundreds of films, and is still active in 1994.

(Courtesy of the Gene Autry Western Heritage Museum.)

The Real McCoy

Military officer, actor, rancher, and cowboy poet Tim McCoy wore this flat-crowned beige felt hat, with ribbon brim edging and ribbon around the base of the crown, in frontier films in the 1930s. Normally, he sported a tall crowned hat of his own design. Written inside the crown in black ink is the inscription "McCoy, No. 1 MGM." Maker unknown–probably Stetson.

(Courtesy of the Gene Autry Western Heritage Museum.)

Guy Madison's 3X Beaver Resistol

This handsome, grey, 3X beaver with rolled brim sides has a pinched crown at left, right, and front, with a deep crease on top. The sweatband is stamped "Resistol 'Self-Conforming' XXX Beaver Nudie's Rodeo Tailors North Hollywood, California." A stetson label appears inside the fully lined crown. The hat was used by Guy Madison, remembered as the actor who portrayed Wild Bill Hickock in the television series of the same name.

(Courtesy of the Gene Autry Western Heritage Museum.)

Clayton Moore's "Lone Ranger" Hat

This light tan Resistol has a pointed front crown in a soft triangular shape, curled brim, and black braided-leather chin strap. This hat, judging by size, color, and style, was worn by Clayton Moore in his role as the *Lone Ranger* in the television and film era of the mid-1950s. The black chin strap is characteristic of the time period and is perhaps the best example of a *Lone Ranger* hat known.

(Courtesy of the Gene Autry Western Heritage Museum.)

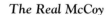

***Cowboy Actor and Actress
Signed Bailey Hat***

Pictured here is a beige Bailey *U Rollit*
straw hat with an oval-shaped crown,
straight sides, dented top, and wide,
turned-up brim. In the crown, seven
open-weave designs serve as air vents, and
around the crown is a brown fabric
hatband. The hat has been signed by
many early cowboy film stars and was
owned by Russell Hayden, the actor who
supported William Boyd in Hoppy films
and who appeared in many western films.
(Courtesy of the Gene Autry Western Heritage Museum.)

The Bonanza Boys
Michael Landon, Pernell Roberts, Dan Blocker
and Lorne Greene ready for some hat-wearin'
shoot-'em-up action.
(Courtesy of Ritch Rand.)

Glenn Ford
Don't mess with this dude
—both hands are smokin'!
(Courtesy of Ritch Rand.)

Ray Whitley's
White Stetson
This 4X Stetson, made of
white felt, has a wide brim with
upturned sides and a crease in the crown.
It is decorated with a Stetson drawing of a
cowboy and horses, and a grosgrain ribbon
band. Stamped on the inner band are the
words "XXXX Stetson John B. Stetson
Co., 4X Beaver." This signature hat was
worn by Ray Whitley, the singer and
songwriter who co-authored Gene Autry's
key song, *Back In The Saddle Again*. After
Whitley's death, his family passed this hat
on to Forrest White.
(Courtesy of the Gene Autry Western Heritage Museum.)

Las Vegas-style 4X Resistol
This black 4X beaver cowboy hat with its broad brim has a long oval crown, pushed in on either side. The crown crease forms a soft triangle. The hat sports a black grosgrain ribbon hatband, with gold lettering on the sweatband that reads "Resistol 'Self-Conforming' 4X Beaver Made In Texas, USA." A tag identifies this hat as Las Vegas-style.
(Courtesy of the Gene Autry Western Heritage Museum.)

Walter Brennan
Promotional shot for *Rio Bravo*.
(Courtesy of Ritch Rand.)

Billy Stevens' Tan Boss Stetson
Famed bronco rider Billy Stevens wore this Stetson during his days with Buffalo Bill's Wild West Show and the 101 Ranch Wild West Show. This Stetson, *The Boss Raw Edge*, has a domed crown, wide brim with upturned edge, and a tan grosgrain ribbon hatband, which is covered by a leather hatband with grey metal studs. Sold by Geo. L. Griffin & Sons, Boston.
(Courtesy of the Gene Autry Western Heritage Museum.)

Dale Robertson's 7X Beaver Resistol

Resistol created this black *Self-Conforming* 7X beaver hat, custom made for Dale Robertson's use in the television series *Tales of Wells Fargo*. It features a wide brim with upturned sides, oval indented crown, and a sterling hatband with buckle (floral design). Stamped inside are the words "Made Especially for Dale Robertson."

(Courtesy of the Gene Autry Western Heritage Museum.)

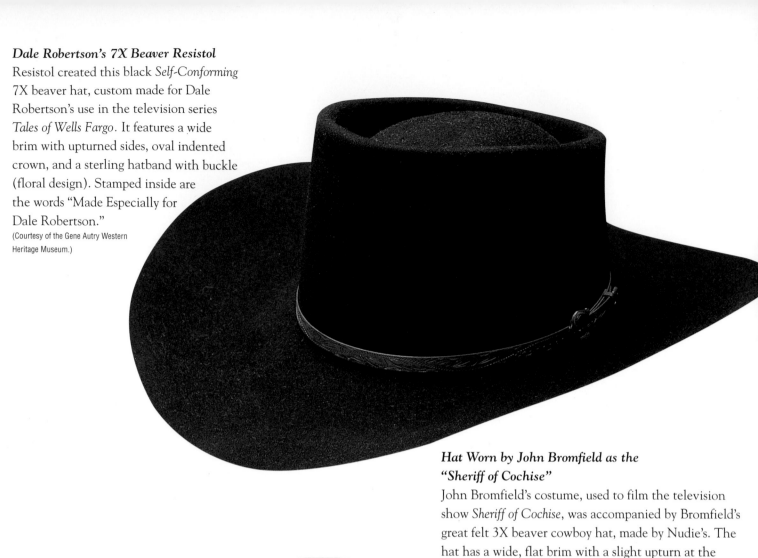

Hat Worn by John Bromfield as the "Sheriff of Cochise"

John Bromfield's costume, used to film the television show *Sheriff of Cochise*, was accompanied by Bromfield's great felt 3X beaver cowboy hat, made by Nudie's. The hat has a wide, flat brim with a slight upturn at the front, an indented crown, a plain brown leather hatband, and is edged with tan grosgrain ribbon.

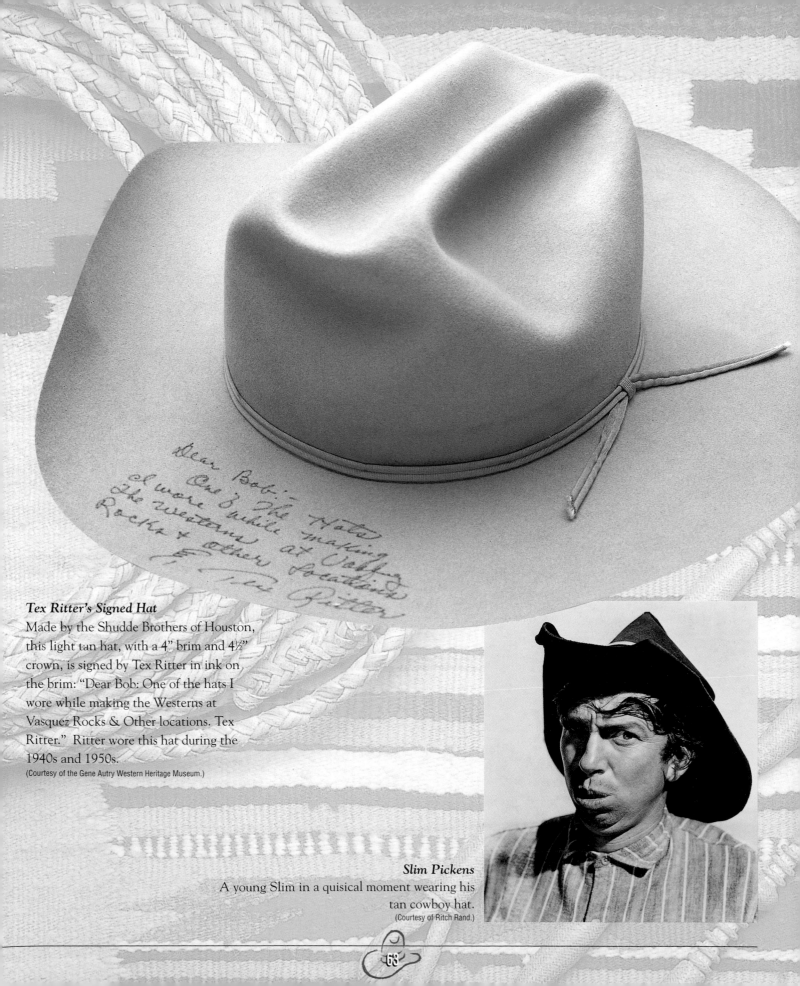

Tex Ritter's Signed Hat
Made by the Shudde Brothers of Houston, this light tan hat, with a 4" brim and 4½" crown, is signed by Tex Ritter in ink on the brim: "Dear Bob: One of the hats I wore while making the Westerns at Vasquez Rocks & Other locations. Tex Ritter." Ritter wore this hat during the 1940s and 1950s.
(Courtesy of the Gene Autry Western Heritage Museum.)

Slim Pickens
A young Slim in a quisical moment wearing his tan cowboy hat.
(Courtesy of Ritch Rand.)

Bat Masterson Hat
This black felt promotional child's hat has a round crown, upward curved brim with vinyl binding, decorative black-and-gold elastic hatband, and *Bat Masterson* character emblem on the front. The banner in front of the emblem reads "Bat Masterson." The inner sweatband reads "An Officially Licensed Hat Tex-Felt T. M. by Arlington, New York 60% Wool, 40% Rayon All New Felt."
(Courtesy of the Gene Autry Western Heritage Museum.)

James Garner
By any other name–Maverick.
(Courtesy of Ritch Rand.)

James Arness' Custom-made Stetson

As Matt Dillon, James Arness wore this custom-made Stetson during the filming of *Gunsmoke*. The light brown felt hat has a grosgrain ribbon hatband and brim edging, with a curved lip on the brim. On the leather sweatband, in gold lettering is the inscription "John B. Stetson Company 3X Beaver XXX Made by Stetson Especially for James Arness." A paper tag has been pinned to the sweatband, and reads "Jim Arness Newest Hat as of 12/21/73." Instantly recognizable!

(Courtesy of the Gene Autry Western Heritage Museum.)

Doc Carver's Stetson

This nutria fur Stetson with a Montana Peak crown and flat brim has tan grosgrain brim edging and hatband, with an added leather hatband. The hat was used by champion rifle shot and Wild West showman Doc Carver in the 1890s.

(Courtesy of the Gene Autry Western Heritage Museum.)

G. Henry Stetson's Stetson

This handsome Stetson 100X, in grey-brown felt, was owned and worn by John B. Stetson's son, G. Henry Stetson. The tall crown is creased down the center with indentations at the front, and the 3½" brim is turned up slightly on the sides. Grey grosgrain ribbon is used along the brim edge and as the hatband. Stamped inside the band is the inscription "G. Henry Stetson." Henry remained active in the Stetson Company for many years. This hat was made for him in the late 1940s.

(Courtesy of the Gene Autry Western Heritage Museum.)

Chuck Connors & Johnny Crawford
Looking good as *The Rifleman*.
(Courtesy of Ritch Rand.)

Chuck Connors' Film-Used Hat
This hat has seen plenty of "Action!"
Used by Chuck Connors in the films
Braided and *Ride Beyond Vengeance*, it is
made of brown suede with braided
leather trim and buckle. The liner at the
crown reads "CC Beaver." The label
under the crown reads "M.L. Eddy Saddle
and Boot Shop, San Angelo—Fort
Worth—Midland, Texas."
(Courtesy of the Gene Autry Western Heritage Museum.)

Charles Starrett
Classic bad guy
(Courtesy of Rich Rand.)

Fabulous Tooled-Leather Cowboy Hat
Unusual and impressive tooled-leather
cowboy hat with high crown indented on
four sides to form a Montana Peak crease,
and a 3¼" stiff, flat brim. Leather hat band
and fully lined, made by CP Shipley of
Kansas City circa 1940. Stunning!
(Courtesy of the Gene Autry Western Heritage Museum.)

Texas Centennial Hat

This beige-colored hat has a deeply creased, oval-shaped crown, and a 3½" brim that is sharply turned up at the edges. Stenciled above the beige grosgrain ribbon hatband on the sides of the hat are the words "Texas 1836–1936 Centennial." The inner band reads "Made in Texas with Texas wool." The fairgrounds in Dallas played host to many elements of celebration for the state's 100th Anniversary in 1936. Tourists and Texas patriots could collect souvenirs of many kinds, including this inexpensive cowboy hat.
(Courtesy of the Gene Autry Western Heritage Museum.)

The Duke and Sidekick Ricky Nelson
A scene from *Rio Bravo*.
(Courtesy of Ritch Rand.)

Hopalong Cassidy
One of Western Americana's most highly prized collectibles; this authentic "Hoppy" hat—an exact replica of Bill " Hopalong Cassidy" Boyd's hat sold during the early fifties for around $2.00! Made by the Bailey Hat Company, this hat is almost impossible to find in a condition as good as this one!
(Courtesy of Ritch Rand.)

Steve McQueen
Steve, packin' his "mare's leg convincer," obviously meant business in *Wanted Dead or Alive*.
(Courtesy of Ritch Rand.)

Guy Madison
Wearing his *Wild Bill Hickock* hat.
(Courtesy of Ritch Rand.)

3X Beaver Stetson
This attractive white beaver 3X Stetson features a crease along the top and sides of the crown, with a broad brim upturned at the edges. It has a matching grosgrain ribbon hatband and brim edging.
(Courtesy of the Gene Autry Western Heritage Museum.)

A Couple of Great 50s "Dude Ranch Hats"
Worn by the ladies, these inexpensive, felt hats feature wide ribbon bands with bound edges. The hats feature similar low creases, typical of this era, sometimes called "Roping Horse Crease."
Note the hat on the right features a "Princess Back Bow" detail.
(Courtesy of Ritch Rand.)

Wild Bill Elliot
Wild Bill Elliot as Red Ryder in
The San Antonio Kid
(Courtesy of Ritch Rand.)

Jack Case's Resistol

This Resistol 3X beaver was used by Jack Case in the last years of the 101 Wild West Show. It has a cream-colored, high-domed crown with a deep front crease, four metal grommets on the sides of the crown, a cream-colored grosgrain ribbon hatband, and brim edging. Unusual and attractive!

(Courtesy of the Gene Autry Western Heritage Museum.)

Buck Jones' Stetson

This one's purtier than a speckled pup! This felt Stetson has a flat, wide brim with curved-up edges trimmed with tan ribbon. The wide tan ribbon hatband has a small horseshoe decoration attached to the band on the right—on the left the ribbon is formed into a bow. The leather sweatband bears a gold-embossed Stetson logo and the words "marketed by C. P. Shipley." The hat is lined with pale yellow material with the Stetson Company crest. The BEST!

(Courtesy of the Gene Autry Western Heritage Museum.)

Ken Maynard
Wearing his version of the Montana Peak.
(Courtesy of the Phil Spangenberger Collection.)

3X Beaver Stetson
This tan, 3X beaver Stetson with an oval-shaped crown has a crease extending from front to back. The 3½" brim is turned up on the sides, and a narrow, brown grosgrain ribbon forms the hatband (and is also found under the brim edges). The maker is Stetson, American Royal Brand, for Chas. P. Shipley Co., Kansas City.
(Courtesy of the Gene Autry Western Heritage Museum.)

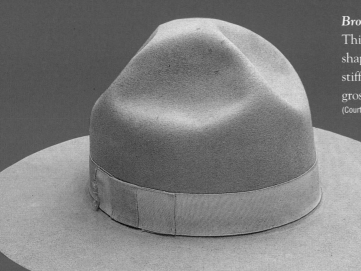

Brown, Flat-Brimmed Cowboy Hat

This unmarked brown hat has an oval-shaped crown with a Montana Peak and a stiff, flat, 3⅓" brim. It sports a tan grosgrain ribbon hatband.
(Courtesy of the Gene Autry Western Heritage Museum.)

"Put It Back…" Stetson

Fred Barrows bought his Stetson from the N. Porter Saddle & Harness Co., of Phoenix and Tucson, and had the following message stamped on the sweatband: "Fred Barrows PUT IT BACK, YOU BASTARD." Fred probably had his hat stolen in the past and figured this was as good a way as any to keep his current Stetson safe! It has a high, conical crown with a deep, forward-sloping crease, a wide (4") near-flat brim with sharply upturned edges, and a beige grosgrain ribbon hatband.
(Courtesy of the Gene Autry Western Heritage Museum.)

Classic Navajo Bailey

A 1970s Bailey *Natani*, this hat is made of pressed black felt with a high, straight-sided, domed crown and a stiff 4" brim. Around the crown is a beautiful Navajo silver hatband with a rope motif. On both sides are butterfly ornaments, and at the center, a many-petaled flower. The tips of the butterfly wings and flower petals are accented with teardrop-shaped pieces of turquoise. Stamped on the inner band is the inscription "Many Farms Trading Post Many Farms, Arizona." This one's a classic!
(Courtesy of the Gene Autry Western Heritage Museum.)

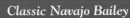

J.C. Penney 3X Beaver

Made by J. C. Penney and Marathon Hats,
this grey-brown 3X beaver cowboy hat
features a high crown with a
forward-dipping crease, a 3½" brim that is
turned up at the edges and rolled on the
sides, and a tan grosgrain ribbon band.
Imprinted in the crown are the words
"J.C. Penney No. 1 Special Quality."
(Courtesy of the Gene Autry Western Heritage Museum.)

Beaver Stetson Made For Ken Maynard

Movie fans will recognize this absolutely terrific hat, even without the face! Custom made for cowboy star Ken Maynard by Stetson, this black, 3X beaver hat features a wide brim with curled edges, a black silk headband, a red interior lining, and a brown leather sweatband. Stamped on the band is the inscription "Made by John B. Stetson Company Especially for Ken Maynard." Also stamped are the words "California Clothing Co. 126 South Main St., Los Angeles." Finally, the Stetson Company has added its own stamp/logo: "John B. Stetson Company—3X beaver, kettle finish, boss raw edge." It's one of the nicest Stetsons we've seen.

(Courtesy of the Gene Autry Western Heritage Museum.)

Tim McCoy

This book wouldn't be complete without a shot of cowboy actor Tim McCoy, wearing his custom-made monster-peaked hat from the mid-1930s.

(Courtesy of Ritch Rand.)

Andy Devine's *Wild Bill Hickock* **Hat**
This beige felt, Resistol hat features a simple, beige, grosgrain piping hatband and brown leather sweatband with a gilded label that reads "Nudie's Rodeo Tailors." It was used by Andy Devine in his role as Jingles Jones in the *Wild Bill Hickock* television series.
(Courtesy of the Gene Autry Western Heritage Museum.)

Brown Stetson Cowboy Hat
This brown cowboy hat by J. B. Stetson Co., for E. C. Olson Company of Rapid City, South Dakota, features a deep frontal crease, a brim turned up at the edges, and a beige ribbon hatband.
(Courtesy of the Gene Autry Western Heritage Museum.)

Henry Fonda
A still from *The Ox-Bow Incident*.
(Courtesy of Ritch Rand.)

Buck Jones
Another star in the Hollywood firmament of cowboy stars.
(Courtesy of Ritch Rand.)

Tom Mix's Hat
Pictured above is one of the Stetsons worn by Tom Mix, arguably the greatest movie cowboy of all time. Made of light tan felt, it features a high crown with indentations on two sides, a 4½" brim with turned up edges, and a black-and-white, braided horsehair hatband. Mix gave this hat as a gift to fellow actor Glen Strange, who later acted as the barkeeper on *Gunsmoke*.
(Courtesy of the Gene Autry Western Heritage Museum.)

Montana Peak Stetson
Four crown indentations form the classic Montana Peak-style hat, 3½" brim, and ribbon hatband. The Stetson mark is on the left side of the sweatband, and gold stamping on the right side of the sweatband reads "Phelps Dodge Mercantile Co. Quality Guaranteed No. 1 Quality Stetson."
(Courtesy of the Gene Autry Western Heritage Museum.)

Gene Autry's 3X Beaver Stetson
This white, Sierra-style Stetson, 3X beaver, was custom made for Gene Autry and features an unblocked crown, a wide brim with slightly upturned edge, and a white grosgrain hatband. A small, sterling-silver stickpin shaped like a cowboy is attached to the knot. Autry wore many types of creases in his cowboy hats over the years, this style being one of the most familiar. It's a perfect reminder that good guys wear white!
(Courtesy of the Gene Autry Western Heritage Museum.)

Wallace Beery's Hat

In 1957, Beery gave this tan cowboy hat to a friend. It features a large-weave fabric sweatband and a narrow, dark brown ribbon hatband. On the 6" crown are several crude ink sketches of Indian items and the following notation (errors intact): "Donated to Robert Callahan by Wallace Berry movie starr 1957."
(Courtesy of the Gene Autry Western Heritage Museum.)

Joel McCrae
The quintessential laid-back cowboy in an open-weave straw hat.
(Courtesy of Ritch Rand.)

Ken Curtis' Gunsmoke *Hat*

Who doesn't recognize this one? Worn by Ken Curtis as Festus Haggen in the TV series *Gunsmoke*, it's made of tan felt and has a rounded crown, a rolled brim, and a leather hatband, distressed by experience.
(Courtesy of the Gene Autry Western Heritage Museum.)

Actor Jimmy Stewart
Stewart's hat displays the essence of today's "distressed" look in high-end hats.
(Courtesy of Ritch Rand.)

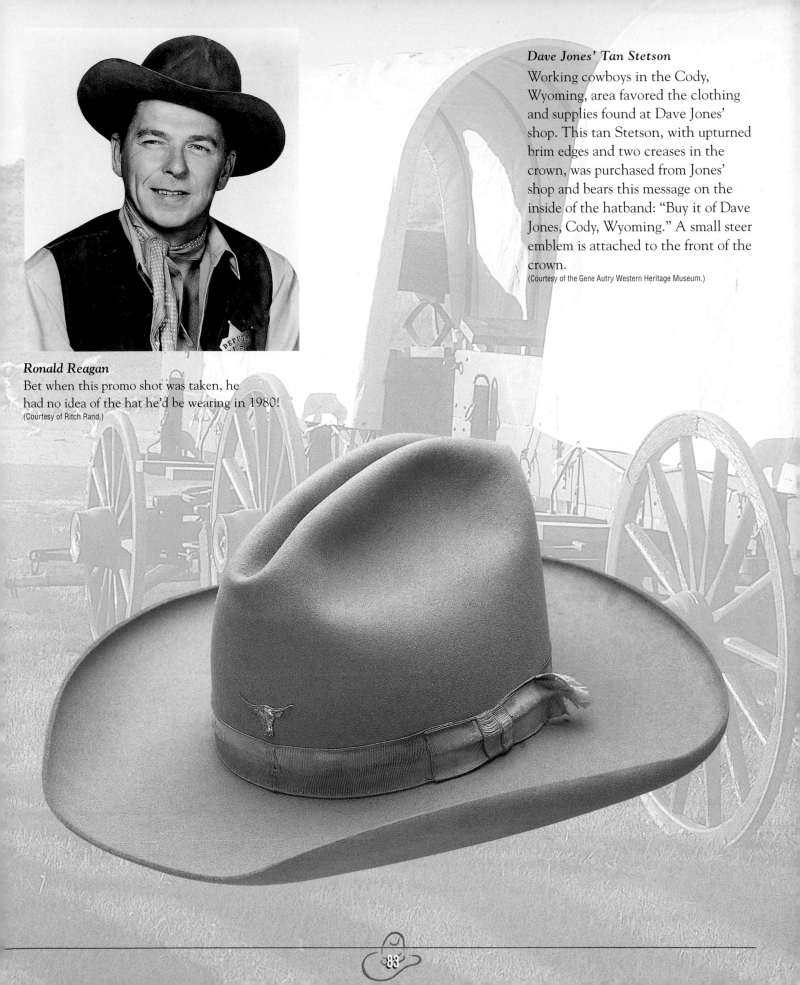

Dave Jones' Tan Stetson

Working cowboys in the Cody, Wyoming, area favored the clothing and supplies found at Dave Jones' shop. This tan Stetson, with upturned brim edges and two creases in the crown, was purchased from Jones' shop and bears this message on the inside of the hatband: "Buy it of Dave Jones, Cody, Wyoming." A small steer emblem is attached to the front of the crown.
(Courtesy of the Gene Autry Western Heritage Museum.)

Ronald Reagan

Bet when this promo shot was taken, he had no idea of the hat he'd be wearing in 1980!
(Courtesy of Ritch Rand.)

A Complete Bohlin Stetson
This classic Stetson is a true "cowboy crown." It features a tooled silver band-and-buckle set by master craftsman Edward H. Bohlin. Circa 1941, this Stetson was sold from Bohlin's shop, as the sweatband and lining indicates.
(Courtesy of the Gene Autry Western Heritage Museum.)

Gary Cooper
Everyone's idea of the strong, silent type.
His hat speaks volumes.
(Courtesy of Ritch Rand.)

Clint Eastwood
Classic Clint as he appeared in *Pale Rider*.
(Courtesy of Ritch Rand.)

Hispanic Style Cowboy Hat
Another example of a richly decorated, Hispanic-style cowboy hat, this one is made of woven plant fiber and painted yellow-white. It has a very wide brim (over 4½") that is turned up at the edges, one side more than the other. The brim edge is covered in brown felt and orange cording, and the indented crown has an elaborately decorated hatband festooned with cording, rickrack, sequins, and small pieces of plastic. The model name is "La Guadalupana."
(Courtesy of the Gene Autry Western Heritage Museum.)

Harry Carey, Jr.
One of Hollywood's most resilient western stars.
(Courtesy of Ritch Rand.)

Hirshfeld's Stetson

This handsome, off-white Stetson with grosgrain ribbon hatband and brim edging was sold by Hirshfeld's Mercantile of Los Angeles. The purple silk lining is stunning.
(Courtesy of the Gene Autry Western Heritage Museum.)

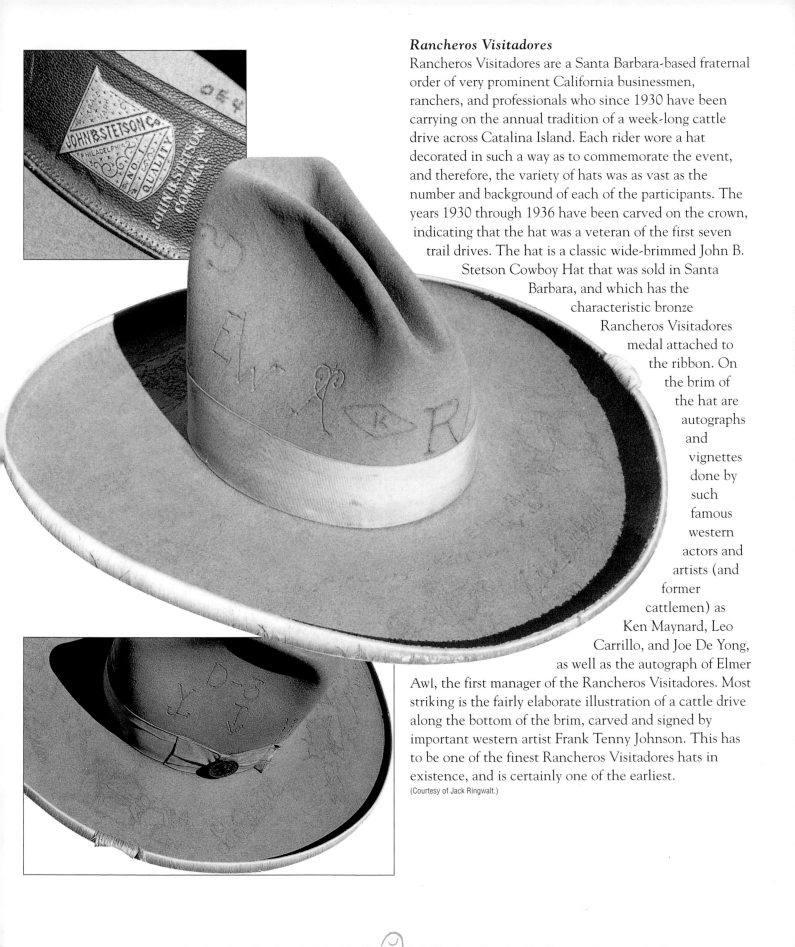

Rancheros Visitadores

Rancheros Visitadores are a Santa Barbara-based fraternal order of very prominent California businessmen, ranchers, and professionals who since 1930 have been carrying on the annual tradition of a week-long cattle drive across Catalina Island. Each rider wore a hat decorated in such a way as to commemorate the event, and therefore, the variety of hats was as vast as the number and background of each of the participants. The years 1930 through 1936 have been carved on the crown, indicating that the hat was a veteran of the first seven trail drives. The hat is a classic wide-brimmed John B. Stetson Cowboy Hat that was sold in Santa Barbara, and which has the characteristic bronze Rancheros Visitadores medal attached to the ribbon. On the brim of the hat are autographs and vignettes done by such famous western actors and artists (and former cattlemen) as Ken Maynard, Leo Carrillo, and Joe De Yong, as well as the autograph of Elmer Awl, the first manager of the Rancheros Visitadores. Most striking is the fairly elaborate illustration of a cattle drive along the bottom of the brim, carved and signed by important western artist Frank Tenny Johnson. This has to be one of the finest Rancheros Visitadores hats in existence, and is certainly one of the earliest.

(Courtesy of Jack Ringwalt.)

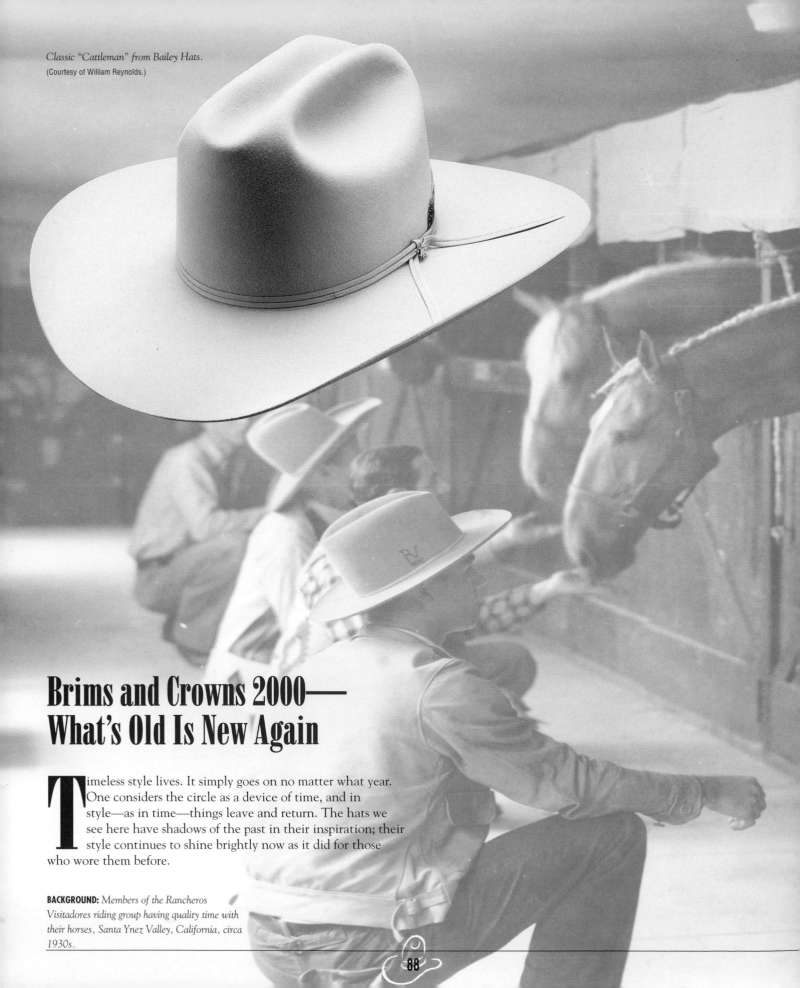

Classic "Cattleman" from Bailey Hats.
(Courtesy of William Reynolds.)

Brims and Crowns 2000— What's Old Is New Again

Timeless style lives. It simply goes on no matter what year. One considers the circle as a device of time, and in style—as in time—things leave and return. The hats we see here have shadows of the past in their inspiration; their style continues to shine brightly now as it did for those who wore them before.

BACKGROUND: *Members of the Rancheros Visitadores riding group having quality time with their horses, Santa Ynez Valley, California, circa 1930s.*

Tom Mix and his Stetson "Boss of the Plains." Elegant is as elegant does.
(Mark Allen Collection, Dickinson Research Center, National Cowboy and Western Heritage Museum, circa 1930s.)

7X, beaded brim and band, black beauty from Spirits in the Wind Gallery.
(Courtesy of Studio Seven.)

The Ladies Who Launch: *Three daring bucking-horse riders from the early Wild West shows, all generating a lot of "shade" with their authentic "Boss of the Plains" hats. From left: Kitty Canutt, Prairie Rose and Ruth Rorch.* (Courtesy William Reynolds.)

Pure beaver hat with laced brim and hair-on-calf band with concho. The crown features a sharp little steer-head cutout. Shorty's Caboy Hattery. (Courtesy of Studio Seven)

Outlaw headwear in
dubious shapes, 1975 style.
Sam Waterston and Jeff
Bridges in Rancho Deluxe.
(Photo courtesy of William
Reynolds.)

The ultimate black hat:
Resistol's 25th anniversary
"Black Gold."
(Courtesy of Studio Seven.)

"Tom Horn" model, with
original drawing by cowboy artist
Larry Bute. Hat by Ritch Rand.
This hat shape has become
known today as the "Tom Horn
Crown."
(Courtesy of Ritch Rand.)

Steve McQueen, creating a style
as legendary as the character he
played—Tom Horn.
(Courtesy of Ritch Rand.)

"Come back, Shane!"
Alan Ladd as Shane,
with costume and hat
designed by Joe De Yong.
(Courtesy of Ritch Rand.)

Joe De Yong burning a design on a hat.
(Courtesy of the Santa Barbara Historical Society.)

Classic "Cattleman" from
M.L. Leddy, direct from the
Stockyards of Ft. Worth,
Texas.
(Courtesy of Studio Seven.)

Robert Redford as Tom Booker in The Horse Whisperer.
(Publicity photo/Touchstone Pictures.)

Stetson Hats swings for the bleachers with its 1000X beaver-and-chinchilla model. Now that's a hat!
(Courtesy of Studio Seven.)

A modified "Gus" shape from the Greeley Hat Works with laced, rolled brim and sterling-silver-and-turquoise band.
(Courtesy of Studio Seven.)

Tom Selleck and Sam Elliott with looks that freeze, from The Sacketts.
(Courtesy of Ritch Rand .)

The "Vaquero" model is very popular with high-desert types and Pacific Slope horsemen. Flat, bound brim with a telescope crown—very cool. Priest Hat Company.
(Courtesy of Studio Seven.)

Style is as style does: Duncan Renaldo as the Cisco Kid.
(Courtesy of Ritch Rand.)

The boys of Tombstone *heading for history: Val Kilmer, Sam Elliott, Kurt Russell and Bill Paxton.*
(Courtesy of Ritch Rand.)

Contrasting bound edge and band make this 20X "Santa Fe" by Ritch Rand.
(Courtesy of Studio Seven.)

The Headwear of State—Hats off to U.S. Presidents and Their Hats

Hats and U.S. presidents have been setters of style since George Washington. A fact that seemed to end with the election of John Kennedy (size 7⁵/₈) as our 35th president in 1961. The coming of Camelot held more in store than just the Bay of Pigs; it was the end of men wearing hats as a broad fashion staple. Good hair replaced great hats. The fedora fell away to the back of the closet. Presidents after Kennedy tried as they could, regionally, to continue the tradition. Lyndon Johnson carried off a classic Texas feel with his Stetson "Open Road," and Ronald Reagan, the "Cowboy President," wore his cowboy hat with

pride. Later hats were made and presented to both Presidents George Bush and George W. Bush. Only George W., though, can be seen regularly wearing his cowboy hat on his ranch in Crawford, Texas. It is a hopeful sign that headwear will return to the oval office and the "ovals" of men everywhere.

Speaking of *oval*, it is a relative term in headwear when it comes to head shapes. Look at this chart of some past presidents: they are anything but oval. And just so your hat information file will be brimming, we include a handy list of many former presidents' head sizes—stuff we feel you should know!

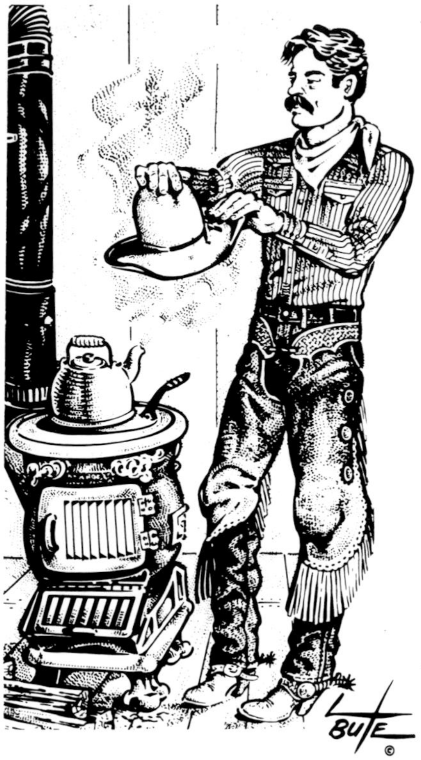

Head size in inches	Head size in centimeters	American hat sizes
19 3/8"	49.2 cm	6 - 1/8
19 1/2"	49.5 cm	6 - 1/4
20 1/4"	51.4 cm	6 - 3/8
20 3/4"	52.7 cm	6 - 1/2
21"	53.3 cm	6 - 5/8
21 1/2"	54.6 cm	6 - 3/4
21 5/8"	54.9 cm	6 - 7/8
22 1/8"	56.2 cm	7
22 1/2"	57.2 cm	7 - 1/8
23"	58.4 cm	7 - 1/4
23 3/8"	59.3 cm	7 - 3/8
23 3/4"	60.3 cm	7 - 1/2
24 1/2"	62.2 cm	7 - 5/8
25"	63.5 cm	7 - 3/4

Head Sizes of Presidents and Well-known Men for the Past 100 Years

Chester A. Arthur....7¼
Fred Astaire.............. 7⅛
Enrico Caruso........... 7¼
Winston Churchill... 7⅛
Grover Cleveland.... 7½
Calvin Coolidge...... 7⅛
Thomas E. Dewey.... 7⅜
Dwight Eisenhower.. 7¼
Henry Ford............... 6⅞
James A. Garfield.....7¾
Ulysses S. Grant......... 7⅜
Warren G. Harding.....7⅜
Benjamin Harrison.....7½
Rutherford B. Hayes...7⅙
J. Edgar Hoover.......... 7½
Herbert Hoover.......... 7⅜
Andrew Johnson........ 7¼
Lyndon B. Johnson.....7⅜
John F. Kennedy..........7⅝
Abraham Lincoln.......7⅛
William McKinley..... 7⅛
Richard M. Nixon..... 7½
Franklin Roosevelt.... 7⅜
Theodore Roosevelt.. 7⅜
Babe Ruth.................. 7½
William Taft...............7¾
Harry S. Truman........ 7⅜
Woodrow Wilson.......7¼
Duke of Windsor........6¾

AT LEFT: *Hat size chart. There's more to fitting a hat than meets the eye. Here's everything you would ever want to know.*
(Courtesy of Bailey Hat Co.)

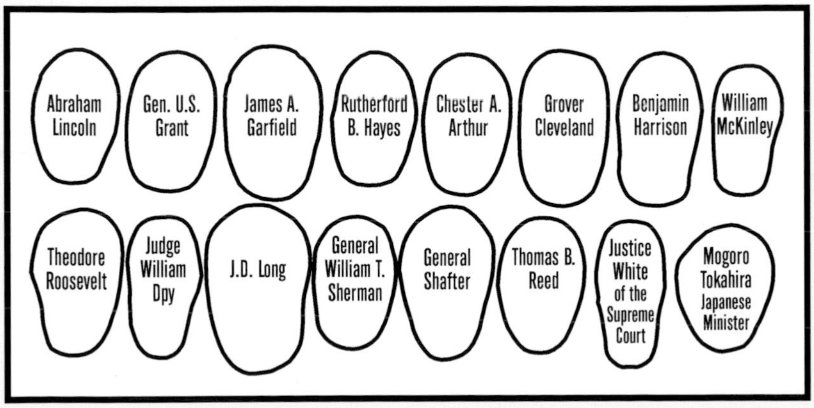

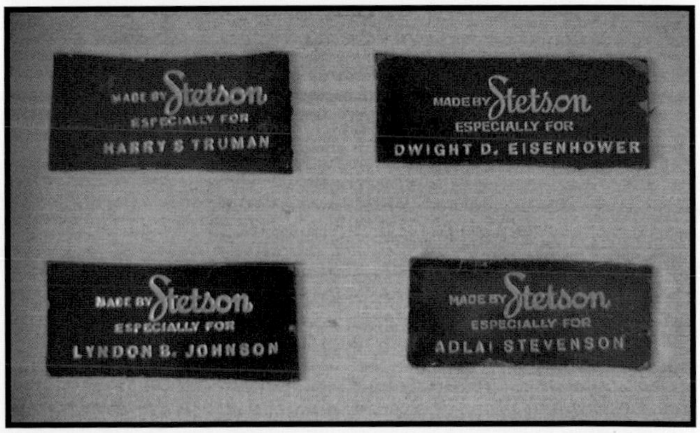

BELOW LEFT: *Head size chart of presidents.*
(Courtesy of Stetson.)

BELOW : *Vintage presidential sweatband labels.*
(Courtesy of Stetson.)

PRESENTED
BY
JACK W. PILLE
SANTA BARBARA

The Importance of Being Earnest—in the West

With apologies to Mr. Wilde. There are those few that cast shadows that others could not ever seem to fill. Those who affected our perception of the West in such a glorious and indelible way as to change us forever. To our good fortune, they all wore hats that spoke volumes about them and their visions. Imagine now being in a room with them—Charles M. Russell, Will James, Joe De Yong and Edward Borein—having them all to yourself. What a moment. The West would not only live but rise in a crescendo of passion and float on a sea of enthusiasm like a feather in the wind. It would be grand!

Charles M. Russell, cowboy artist and painter of sunsets.
(Courtesy of John T. Reynolds.)

Edward Borein working on his miniature saddlery
(Courtesy of Harold Davidson.)

MADE BY
JOHN B. STETSON COMPANY
ESPECIALLY FOR
ED. BOREIN

Joe De Yong, the only apprentice to cowboy artist Charles M. Russell, working in Hollywood as a costume and set-design artist during the golden age of the Western.
(Photo courtesy of the Santa Barbara Historical Society.)

The Boys: Charles M. Russell with John Edward Borein.
(Courtesy of the Santa Barbara Historical Society.)

CENTER LEFT: *Will James as a star, 1931.*
(Joe De Yong Collection, Dickinson Research Center, National Cowboy and Western Heritage Museum.)

Edward Borein's Stetson hat and inscribed sweatband.
(Courtesy Reynolds Family Collection.)

Riding Straight Up: Getting big air with the aid of one's hat.

(Ralph R. Doubleday, courtesy of William Reynolds.)

Hat Fanning: The End of an Era

Over the years hats have provided more than just shade. Everything from a bucket to a feed bag has been fashioned from a lineage of trusty chapeaus. As the twentieth century progressed, machines found their way into the lives of farmers and ranchers, separating them from livestock as implements. Rodeos and stock shows kept the public in touch with animals and the need for excitement grew with the diversity of the crowd. Bucking horses needed to buck harder.

Fanning, or the waving of one's hat, added to the moment by spooking the horse on to a more "colorful" ride. It worked.

Today, horses for rodeo are bred to buck and horsemen in general would prefer a more comfortable ride. The need for "big air" to impress one's pals has passed, and along with it, the hat fan.

Thank goodness.

Lest We Forget

Consider the effects of those who have gone before. Arguably the folks on this page created a genre that will last forever. They did it with such skill and grace that the mere mention of their first names is enough. They created permission for millions of people to don their cowboy hats and ride off to a simpler time. Roy and Dale, Gene and Hoppy, happy trails to you and all of us.

TOP: *Roy Rogers, the reigning king of all our happy trails.*
(Courtesy of Ritch Rand.)

ABOVE: *Dale Evans, always the Queen of the West.*
(Courtesy of Ritch Rand.)

LEFT: *Gene Autry, the "singing cowboy," who won the world and finally the baseball World Series with a team of Angels.*
(Courtesy of William Reynolds.)

BACKGROUND: *William Boyd as Hoppy. The Bar 20 was always just over the rise, but home felt close. Our hero in basic black.*
(Courtesy of Ritch Rand.)

Hat Etiquette

It is probably best to consider your cowboy hat as a living entity; it should be treated with care accordingly.

Classic examples:

Do not leave your cowboy hat in the back window of your car while parked out in the heat of the day.

Do not leave your cowboy hat in the trunk of your car while parked out in the heat of the day.

Better yet, don't leave your hat in the car at all.

It has always been considered bad luck to place your cowboy-hat brim on the bed.
(The origin of this wisdom is a bit cloudy.)

When looking for a place to put your cowboy hat, the first and most appropriate spot is on top of your head.

When entering an enclosed living space, such as a home, it is proper to remove one's hat. This does not count for barns and bars, only places where people reside.

★

A gentleman always removes his hat when first meeting a lady. In subsequent meetings, the gentleman tips his hat to the lady.

Our language is peppered with hat talk, and as hats gained in popularity, they became well-known metaphors. Even if you owned only one hat, you could take the latest gossip and "keep it under your hat." You might "take your hat off" to a hero, "throw your hat in the air" to celebrate, or "throw your hat into the ring" to enter some sort of competition. To make a friend comfortable in your home, you'd invite him to "hang your hat anywhere." If you don't know what you're saying, you're "talking through your hat." A drunk "had a brick in his hat." A "bad hat" was a bad man, and once western movies came along, everyone knew the good guys from the bad guys by their white hats. "Hang on to your hat" because any of these phrases could change "at the drop of a hat." Need to buy yourself a new hat? Try

White Hats Rule in Calgary

In Calgary, home of the Calgary Stampede, a white cowboy hat is a metaphor for the city and its people. Visitors can become honorary Calgarians through a unique presentation where they receive a white cowboy hat and take a pledge agreeing to spread Calgary's brand of hospitality around the world.

The tourism bureau also holds an annual White Hat Award ceremony, where employees from the hospitality industry are presented with the traditional white hat in recognition of outstanding service.

If you want to have a White Hat Ceremony for yourself or friends, go to visitor.calgary.ab.ca/travel/whitehat.html.

And if you care to nominate your favorite hotel clerk or restaurant waitress for a White Hat Award, fill out the form at tourismcalgary.com/ccvb/whitehatnominate2002.html.

"passing the hat." Or take your chances in a game of risk by "betting your hat." Anyone who is absolutely sure about something is known to claim "I'll eat my own hat." Some hats became trademarks—"high hats," "brass hats," "hard hats," even "wool hats," a term for bumpkins. Finally, for the sports fan, there was the rare "hat trick"—three goals in a single game (the term originated with British cricket when three goals in one game would win the player a hat from the local club).

But hat wearing does have its difficult moments, especially when one goes indoors into a public establishment. The hat wearer is faced not only with the "etiquette" question of whether or not to remove the hat, but also with the bigger dilemma of what to do with the hat once it's removed . Where does one place it safely?

What has taken place in the course of the last thirty years in this country is the loss of restaurants and hotels that offer cloakrooms—places where one can check one's hat. There is not a chance on this planet that a fellow wearing his $300, 20X hat will leave the hat on a peg when he enters a restaurant or theater; nor will he place his hat under a chair. The

world of the cloakroom and its inherent orderliness was a quality of the past that, in this writer's view, is long missed. Now, certainly, some of the finer establishments do offer this time-honored safe haven for your hat, but with the onslaught of fast food establishments, malls, and box stores where space is at a premium, this luxury of personal service for the hat wearer seems to be disappearing.

Probably the biggest problem of all—which has become something of a conceptual dilemma—is what to do with a cowboy hat in an airplane. Airplanes were not designed for people wearing cowboy hats. Flight attendants, when shown a cowboy hat and asked for space to store it, generally suggest the overhead bin, "bin" being the operative word here (most cowboys think of a bin as being a place to store grain). Or they'll suggest putting the hat under the seat in front of the hat wearer. Generally, a person will comply with the attendant's suggestion only once. The condition of the hat at the end of the flight will prove this out. So what do you do with a cowboy hat on a plane? You wear it— either on your head, or for a change of pace, wear it on your knee (this works with all but those hats with the biggest brims and crowns).

Hat Cases and Boxes

Traveling with a hat leads naturally to a discussion of hat boxes and cases. Hat cases have been the easiest and best solution for hat travel for many, many years. The hat case became a necessity for those owning many hats, more than it did for anyone traveling with a hat they weren't currently wearing. Over time, hat cases have not changed much. They're basically containers that give the hat, brim, crown, etc., the proper support and cushioning during travel. Paper boxes were quite the rage at the turn of the century and have evolved over time into today's almost bombproof lockboxes.

The hat box that one receives when purchasing a hat is perfectly serviceable for home use as a place to store the hat during off-season. Hats are seasonal, with felt hats typically being worn during the cooler months and straws being used in the warmer seasons. There are those who, because of geographical and atmospheric conditions, wear felt or straw all year long. The etiquette here is pretty much a personal statement.

ABOVE: *To the left is the Stetson hat case produced for the Stetson 100 anniversary (it cost $100 during the thirties). To protect your top hat during the early 1900s, you most certainly had to have one of these fitted leather cases during your travels. The shape tells it all (case on the right).*

ABOVE: *Stetson produced these classic action hat boxes during the early to mid-1900s. These image-based containers are highly prized by collectors today.*

RIGHT: *An example of classic hat-case packaging with a cowboy campsite scenario from Stetson and Resistol, circa late 1940s, early 1950s.*

ABOVE: *A very special hand-tooled leather hat box made by Ken Griffin for pivotal western figure Gene Autry during the early forties. Notice the detail on the tooled horse heads that adorn the lid.*

LEFT: *Interior detail of the "Stetson 100" hat and its exclusive case.*

RIGHT: *Contemporary hat boxes continue to evoke the spirit and imagery of the Wild West.*

The Cowboy Hat, 2000 and Beyond

SUMMARY

A final thought about cowboy hats. The cowboy hat is the last chance for many of us to be a part of a great adventure. There is a magic moment that happens when someone puts a cowboy hat on for the first time. They are immediately at one with a great adventure—an adventure that took place during a very brief time—the golden age of the cowman and cowboy. That golden age lasted twenty years during the late 1800s, but the legend remains today in the magic of the cowboy and his trappings—and especially in the cowboy hat.

Charles M. Russell at Buffalo Round-up 1908.
(Courtesy Historical Rarities.)

Fur Felt Hat Manufacturers — Finished Hats

Colorado
Greeley Hat Works
725 10th St.
Greeley, CO 80631
(970) 353-7300

Missouri
Stetson Hat Co., Inc.
4500 Stetson Trl.
P.O. Box 1349
St. Joseph, MO 64502
(816) 233-8031

Langenberg Hat Co.
320 W. Front St.
P.O. Box 1860
Washington, MO 63090
(314) 239-1860

Nevada
Keystone Brothers
1848 Deming Way
Sparks, NV 89431
(702) 359-8884

New Jersey
W. Alboum Hat Co.
1439 Springfield Ave.
Irvington, NJ 07111
(201) 371-9100

Modern Hatters
313 Third St.
Jersey City, NJ 07302
(201) 659-9300

New York
Bollman Hat Co.
Suite 1130, Empire State Bldg.
350 Fifth Ave.
New York, NY 10118
(800) 437-0003

Polo Ralph Lauren
650 Madison Ave.
New York, NY 10022
(212) 318-7000

Oklahoma
Shorty's Caboy Hattery
Oklahoma City, OK
(800) 853-4287

Pennsylvania
F&M Hat Co., Inc.
103 Walnut
Denver, PA 17517
(717) 336-5505

Outback Trading Co., Ltd.
39 South Third St.
Oxford, PA 19363
(800) 932-5141

Texas
Bailey Hat Company
3201 NE Loop 820, Ste. 275
Fort Worth, TX 76137-2434
(800) 999-6399

Milano Hat Co., Inc.
10203 Corkwood, Suite 101
Dallas, TX 75238-1200
(214) 342-0071

Hat Brands, Incorporated
(Resistol, Stetson, Charlie 1 Horse)
601 Marion Dr.
Garland, TX 75042
(214) 494-0511

American Hat Co., Inc.
P.O. Box 2808
Conroe, TX 77305
(409) 756-8755

Master Hatters of Texas
2365 Forest Ln.
Garland, TX 75042
(214) 276-4114

Texas Hatters
5003 Overpass
Buda, TX 78610
(512) 295-HATS

Wrangler Hats
2365 Forest Ln.
Garland, TX 75042
(214) 276-4114

Michael Malone
117 Houston St.
Fort Worth, TX 76102
(817) 336-7374

Virginia
Miller Bros. Hat Co.
3301 Castlewood Rd.
Richmond, VA 23234
(804) 233-9683

Wyoming
Jackson Hole Hat Co.
Jackson Hole, WY
(307) 733-7687

Canada
Baltimore Corporation
139 Morris St.
Guelph, Ontario
Canada N1H 6L7
(800) 265-8382

Wool Felt Hat Manufacturers — Finished Hats

California
Golden Gate Hat & Cap Co.
157 South Fairfax Ave.
Los Angeles, CA 90036
(213) 525-1400

Colorado
Greeley Hat Works
725 10th St.
Greeley, CO 80631
(970) 353-7300

Missouri
Langenberg Hat Co.
320 W. Front St.
P.O. Box 1860

Washington, MO 63090
(314) 239-1860

New York
Bollman Hat Co.
Suite 542, Empire State Bldg.
350 Fifth Ave.
New York, NY 10118
(212) 564-6480

Arlington Hat Co., Inc.
4700 Thirty-fourth St.
Long Island City, NY 11101
(718) 361-3000

Oklahoma
Shorty's Caboy Hattery
Oklahoma City, OK
(800) 853-4287

Texas
American Hat Co., Inc.
P.O. Box 2808
Conroe, TX 77305
(409) 756-8755

Bailey Hat Company
3201 NE Loop 820, Ste. 275
Fort Worth, TX 76137-2434
(800) 999-6399

Wyoming
Jackson Hole Hat Co.
Jackson Hole, WY
(307) 733-7687

Canada
Baltimore Corporation
139 Morris St.
Guelph, Ontario
Canada N1H 6L7
(800) 265-8382

Finishers and Renovators

Arizona
Arizona Hatters
3600 N. 1st Ave., #100
Tuscon, AZ 85719
(520) 292-1320

Hirt, Thomas
P.O. Box 31751
Tucson, AZ 85751
(520) 749-5221

California
Paul's Hat Works
6128 Geary Blvd.
San Francisco, CA 94121
(415) 221-5332

Western Hat Works
868 Fifth Ave.
San Diego, CA 92101
(619) 234-0457

Colorado
Greeley Hat Works
725 10th St.
Greeley, CO 80631
(970) 353-7300

O'Farrell Hat Mfg. Co.
563 Main Ave.
Durango, CO 81301
(303) 259-2517

Wimberly's Western Hatter
1315 18½ Rd.
Fruita, CO 81521
(303) 858-1100

Connecticut
Del Monico Hatter
47 Elm St.
New Haven, CT 06510
(203) 787-4086

Florida
Village Cleaners, Inc.
1001 W. 48th St.
Palm Springs Mile,
Hialeah, FL 33012
(305) 821-7951

Idaho
Priest Hat Co.
342 E. State Box 37
Eagle, ID 83610
(208) 939-4287

J.E.T. Hat Cleaners
131 W. Logan St.
Rathdrum, ID 83858

Illinois
Stratton Hats Inc.
3200 Randolph St.
Bellwood, IL 60104
(708) 544-5220

Master Hatters
200 Prairie St.
Rockford, IL 61107

Bond Ave. Hat Works
1903 Bond Ave.
East St. Louis, IL 62207
(618) 874-1715

New World Hat Co.
4146 W. Madison
Chicago, IL 60624
(312) 638-4900

Indiana
Economy Cleaners
354 N. Tibbs
Indianapolis, IN 46222
(317) 634-9262

Maryland
Ecuador Panama Hat Co.
301 W. Fayette St.
Baltimore, MD 21201
(410) 727-5906

Hippodrome Hatters
15 N. Eutaw St.
Baltimore, MD 21201
(410) 727-4287

Massachusetts
Parrott Hatters
73 Middlesex
Lowell, MA 01852
(508) 453-4622

Michigan
Henry The Hatter
1307 Broadway
Detroit, MI 48226
(313) 962-0970

Missouri
Arrow Quality Hat Works
3838 Troost Ave.
Kansas City, MO 64109
(816) 931-2452

Wardrobe Service, Inc.
2908 Main
Kansas City, MO 64108
(816) 753-0033

Montana
Rand's Custom Hatters
2205 1st Ave. North
Billings, MT 59101
(406) 259-4886

New Jersey
Modern Hatters
313 Third St.
Jersey City, NJ 07302
(201) 659-9300

New Mexico
The Montecristi
118 Galisteo St.
Santa Fe, NM 87501
(505) 983-9598

Davis Hats
1510-A Wyoming NE
Albuquerque, NM 87112
(505) 294-7634

The Man's Hat Shop
511 Central NW
Albuquerque, NM 87101
(505) 247-9605

New York
I.M.S. Hats Inc.
2417 Third Ave.
Bronx, NY 10451
(718) 665-2787

Dave Brown The Hatter
3054 W. Henrietta Rd.
Rochester, NY 14623
(716) 475-1791

Albrizio Inc.
30 W. 39th St.
New York, NY 10018
(212) 719-5290

Custom Hatter
1291 Broadway
Buffalo, NY 14212
(716) 896-3722

Ohio
Batsakes Bros.
605 Walnut
Cincinnati, OH 45202
(513) 721-9345

Bill Taylor Hat Co., Inc., The
801 Prospect Ave.
Cleveland, OH 44115
(216) 241-3544

Pennsylvania
Kokoros Hatters
1407 State
Erie, PA 16501
(814) 455-9852

Texas
American Hat Co., Inc.
1505 Porter Rd.
P.O. Box 2808
Houston, TX 77305
(409) 756-8755

Peters Bros. Inc.
909½ Houston St.
Ft. Worth, TX 76102
(817) 335-1715

Keith's Hat Shop
409 E. Main
Alice, TX 78332
(512) 664-3035

Kattan Hat Center
119 W. Jackson Ave.
Harlingen, TX 78550
(210) 425-2575

Johnny's Custom Hatters
211 E. Cotton St.
Longview, TX 75881
(903) 753-4600

Hatatorium
25 N. Chadbourne
San Angelo, TX 76903
(915) 655-9191

Standard Hat Works, Inc.
422 W. Waco Dr.
Waco, TX 76701
(817) 753-5752

Huskey Hat Co.
1225 E. Scott
Wichita Falls, TX 76303
(817) 767-2071

Warnock Hat Works
603 W. Highway
Pharr, TX 78577
(210) 781-1012

Washington
Eclipse Hat Shop
1517 First Ave.
Seattle, WA 98101
(206) 623-2926

Wyoming
Jackson Hole Hat Co.
255 N. Glenwood
Box 1308
Jackson, WY 83001
(307) 733-7687

Weather Hat Co. of WY
1384 Coffeen Ave.
Sheridan, WY 82801
(307) 674-6675

FINISHERS OF FUR FELT HATS

California
Stomper Hats
P.O. Box 1132
Citrus Heights, CA 95611
(916) 782-3500

Colorado
Greeley Hat Works
725 10th St.
Greeley, CO 80631
(970) 353-7300

Missouri
Arrow Quality Hat Works
3838 Troost Ave.
Kansas City, MO 64109
(816) 931-2452

New Jersey
Alboum W. Hat Co., Inc.
1439 Springfield Ave.
Irvington, NJ 07111
(201) 371-9100

Albrizio Inc.
30 W. 39th St.
New York, NY 10018
(212) 719-5290

Dorel Hat Co.
1 Main St.
Beacon, NY 12508
(914) 831-5231

L&G Hat Company, Inc.
10-15 Clintonville St.
Whitestone, NY 11357
(718) 746-0080

Charm Creations Inc.
50 W. 29th St.
New York, NY 10001
(212) 686-9888

Ohio
Batsakes Bros.
605 Walnut
Cincinnati, OH 45202
(513) 721-9345

Texas
Master Hatters of Texas
2365 Forest Ln.
Garland, TX 75042
(214) 276-4114

RENOVATORS OF FELT, PANAMA, STRAW AND SILK HATS

California
Woodard, D.R.
2261 Jay
Sacramento, CA 95816

Carpe, Henry
127 Ocean Ave.
San Francisco, CA 94112

Fifth Avenue Hat Shop
449 N. Edgewood
Inglewood, CA 90302
(213) 678-2479

Colorado
Greeley Hat Works
725 10th St.
Greeley, CO 80631
(970) 353-7300

Florida
Mike's Hat Shop
116 SE First St.
Gainesville, FL 32601

Idaho
Priest Hat Co.
342 E. State Box 37
Eagle, ID 83616
(208) 939-4287

Illinois
Dan's Hat Shop
30 E. Chester
Champaign, IL 61820

Herb The Hatter
540 E. 88th St.
Chicago, IL 60619

Pekin Hatters
4101 S. State St.
Chicago, IL 60609
(312) 268-8200

Indiana
Hoosier Hatters
802 E. Gember
Indianapolis, IN 46203

Victory Cleaners
5924 28 E. 10th
Indianapolis, IN 46219

Louisiana
Conant's Cleaners
1614 Texas St.
Natchitoches, LA 71457
(318) 352-2213

Lee & Son, Hatters
2300 S. Claiborne Ave.
New Orleans, LA 70125
(504) 523-0879

Maryland
American Hatters
9904 Broad St.
Bethesda, MD 20814

Michigan
Jones Bros.
5024 W. Warren Ave.
Detroit, MI 48210

Uptown Hatters & Dry Cleaners
350 Division Ave.
Grand Rapids, MI 49502

Nevada
D Bar J Hat Co.
3873 Spring Mountian Rd.
Las Vegas, NV 89102
(702) 362-4287

New Jersey
Niesenson The Hatter
25 William St.
Newark, NJ 07102
(201) 622-2203

Wyckoff Cleaners
670 Wyckoff
Wyckoff, NJ 07481
(201) 891-0574

New Mexico
Southwest Hatters
1709 N. Solano
Las Crues, NM 88081

New York
Melrose Hat Collection &
Practical Hat Cleaning Co.
124 4th St.
Troy, NY 12180

Ohio
Jack's Hat Cleaning
113 N. Wayne Ave.
Lockland, OH 45215

New Mexico
Nathalie
503 Canyon Rd.
Santa Fe, NM 87501
(505) 982-1021

Oklahoma
John's Hatters & Cleaners
2214 Belleview Terrace
Oklahoma City, OK 73112

Oregon
Crown Cleaners & Laundry
1935 Valley
Baker, OR 97814

Pennsylvania
His & Hers Hats
P.O. Box 87
York, PA 17401

Yorgey's Cleaners & Dryers
Fairview & 17th
Reading, PA 19602

South Dakota
Thelin Cleaners
612 First Ave.
Sisserton, SD 57262

Texas
University Cleaners
112 N. Main
North Gate College Station, TX 77840

Up to Date Cleaners & Hatters
714 W. Gray
Houston, TX 77019

Paris Hatters
119 N. Broadway
San Antonio, TX 78205

Virginia
Crest Cleaners
9048 Mathis Ave.
Manassas, VA 22110

Washington
Vogue Cleaners
3804 Summit View Ave.
Yakima, WA 98902

West Virginia
Sauro's Dry Cleaners
107 Merchant St.
Fairmont, WV 26554

Wisconsin
London Hat Shop
778 N. Milwaukee
Milwaukee, WI 53202
(414) 276-3010

DISTRIBUTORS

California
Leonard Kolber Co., Inc
77547 Michigan Dr.
Palm Desert, CA 92260-8029

Colorado
Greeley Hat Works
725 10th St.
Greeley, CO 80631
(970) 353-7300

Illinois
Star Headwear
2700 N. Elston Ave.
Chicago, IL 60647
(312) 384-2000

Missouri
Lambert MFG. Co., Inc.
P.O. Box 32
Bethany, MO 64424
(816) 425-3213

Lambert MFG Co., Inc.
105 Elm St.
Chilicothe, MO 64601
(800) 821-7667

Lambert MFG Co., Inc.
609 S. Main
Gallatin, MO 64640
(816) 663-2422

New Jersey
Kathy Jeanne, Inc.
51 Sindle Ave.
Little Falls, NJ 07424
(212) 268-5492

New York
F&M Headwear, Inc.
350 5th Ave., Suite 1311
New York, NY 10118
(212) 736-3225

Bollman Hats, Inc
Suite 1130 Empire State Bldg.
350 5th Ave.
New York, NY 10118
(212) 564-6480

J.M. Imports Hats NY
6344 Saunders St.
Rego Park, NY 11374
(718) 997-9827

Biltmore, Inc.
43 West 33rd St.
Room 602
New York, NY 10001
(212) 971-0400

Texas
Sunbeater Co., Inc.
Box 565867
Dallas, TX 75356
(214) 631 0018

HAT MANUFACTURERS BRANCH SALES OFFICES

California
Pacific Sportswear & Emblem
P.O. Box 152111
San Diego, CA 92115
(619) 281-6688

Paul Harris Co
1031-A Calle Trepadora
San Clemente, CA 92673
(714) 493-3743

Colorado
Greeley Hat Works
725 10th St.
Greeley, CO 80631
(970) 353-7300

Missouri
Lambert MFG Co. Inc.
P.O. Box 32
Bethany, MO 64424
(816) 425-3213

Lambert MFG Co., Inc.
105 Elm St.
Chilicothe, MO 64601
(800) 821-7667

Lambert MFG Co. Inc.
609 S. Main
Gallatin, MO 64640
(816) 663-2422

F&M Headwar, Inc.
350 5th Ave., Suite 1311
New York, NY 10118
(212) 736-3225

Bollman Hats, Inc.
Suite 1130 Empire State Bldg.
350 5th Ave.
New York, NY 10118
(212) 564-6480

Head First Co.
990 Avenue of America
Room 5-H
New York, NY 10018
(800) 966-4287

Arlington Hat Co., Inc.
4700 34th St.
Long Island, NY 11101
(212) 683-1155

Sun Yorkos Enterprise
10 E. 39th St. Ste. 533
New York, NY 10016

Stetson Hat Co., Inc.
c/o Paul Guilden
350 5th Ave. Room 1324
New York, NY 10118
(212) 563-3765

Worth & Worth LTD
21 E. 37th St.
New York, NY 10016

Kangol Headwear Inc.
366 Fifth Ave., Ste. 615
New York, NY 10001
(212) 563-0950

Biltmore, Inc.
43 W. 33rd RM 602
New York, NY 10001
(800) 842-3185

Texas
Summit Hat Co.
3401 Gulf Freeway
Houston, TX 77003

EXPORTERS OF HEADWEAR

California
Aegean Headwear
1200 Industrial Rd. #6
San Carlos, CA 94070
(415) 593-8300

Sand Mfg. Corp.
8775 Production Ave.
San Diego, CA 92121
(619) 695-0630

Goorin Bros. Inc.
115 Park Ln.
Brisbane, CA 94005
(415) 467-9195

Ace HY Sales Inc.
21541 Nordhoff St., Bldg. A
Chatsworth, CA 91311
(818) 700-0268

Dorfman Pacific Co. Inc.
P.O. Box 213005
Stockton, CA 95213-9005
(209) 982-1400

California Headwear Inc.
660 S. Myers St.
Los Angeles, CA 90023
(213) 268-7112

Fiesta Fashions
5045 Sixth St.
Carpinteria, CA 93013
(805) 684-7788

Golden Gate Hat Co.
8211 W. 3rd St.
Los Angeles, CA 90048
(213) 525-1400

Colorado
Imperial Headwear Inc.
5200 E. Evans Ave.
Denver, CO 80222
(303) 757-1166

Florida
Manhattan Miami Sales
5019 NW 165th St.
Hialeah, FL 33014
(305) 628-3630

Triangle Sports Headwear
8315 W. 20th Ave.
Hialeah, FL 33014
(305) 558-4310

Illinois
Star Headwear
2700 N. Elston Ave.
Chicago, IL 60647
(312) 384-2000

Kentucky
Town Talk
P.O. Box 58157
Louisville, KY 40268
(502) 933-7575

Derby Cap Mfg.
419 Frenzer Box 34220
Louisville, KY 40232
(502) 587-8495

Massachusetts
Korber Hats, Inc.
P.O. Box 336
Fall River, MA 02724
(800) 428-9911

Universal Industris, Inc.
5 Industrial Dr.
Mattapoisett, MA 02739-0961
(508) 758-6101

Michigan
Broner, Inc.
1750 Harmon Rd.
Auburn Hills, MI 48326
(800) 521-1318

Missouri
Langenberg Hat Co.
320 Front St. Box 1860
Washington, MO 63090
(314) 239-1860

Bee Hat Co.
1021 Washington Ave.
St. Louis, MO 63101
(314) 231-6631

Henschel Mfg. Co.
1706 Olive St.
St. Louis, MO 63103
(314) 421-0010

About The Authors

William C. Reynolds is the Associate Publisher of *Cowboys & Indians* magazine. He is the coauthor of *The Faraway Horses* with horseman Buck Brannaman. He lives with his family and horses in Santa Ynez Valley, California.

Ritch Rand's family has been making quality custom hats in Billings, Montana, for more than twenty years. His handcrafted hats have graced heads of state and Hollywood's most famous. From presidents to kings, Rand's custom hats are worn by both working cowboys and the world's elite.